SAVING THE SCHINDLERS' DAUGHTER

IN MEMORIAM

Atarah, *née* Ben-Tovim

1940-2022

Also by Douglas Boyd
Histories:
April Queen, Eleanor of Aquitaine
Voices from the Dark Years
The French Foreign Legion
The Kremlin Conspiracy: 1,000 years of Russian expansionism
Normandy in the time of Darkness: life and death in the Channel ports 1940-45
Blood in the Snow, Blood on the Grass: treachery and massacre, France 1944
De Gaulle: the man who defied six US presidents
Lionheart: the true story of England's crusader king
The Other First World War: the blood-soaked Russian fronts 1914-22
Daughters of the KGB: Moscow's Cold War spies, sleepers and assassins
Agente – Female spies in World Wars, Cold Wars and Civil Wars
The Solitary Spy
Red October – the revolution that changed the world
Lockerbie – the truth
Moscow Rules
The Plantagenet Princesses
The Plantagenet Princes
Plagues and Pandemics
In preparation: Henry II – England's French king

Novels:
The Eagle and the Snake
The Honour and the Glory
The Truth and the Lies
The Virgin and the Fool
The Fiddler and the Ferret
The Spirit and the Flesh

SAVING THE SCHINDLERS' DAUGHTER

HOW COURAGEOUS WOMEN RESCUED AN ORPHANED GIRL FROM FRENCH CONCENTRATION CAMPS

DOUGLAS BOYD

PEN & SWORD
HISTORY
AN IMPRINT OF PEN & SWORD BOOKS LTD.
YORKSHIRE – PHILADELPHIA

First published in Great Britain in 2023 by
PEN AND SWORD HISTORY
An imprint of
Pen & Sword Books Ltd
Yorkshire – Philadelphia

ISBN 978 1 39906 079 0

A CIP catalogue record for this book is available from the British Library.

Typeset in Times New Roman 12/16 by
SJmagic DESIGN SERVICES, India.
Printed and bound in the UK by CPI Group (UK) Ltd.

Pen & Sword Books Limited incorporates the imprints of Atlas, Archaeology, Aviation, Discovery, Family History, Fiction, History, Maritime, Military, Military Classics, Politics, Select, Transport, True Crime, Air World, Frontline Publishing, Leo Cooper, Remember When, Seaforth Publishing, The Praetorian Press, Wharncliffe Local History, Wharncliffe Transport, Wharncliffe True Crime and White Owl.

For a complete list of Pen & Sword titles please contact
PEN & SWORD BOOKS LIMITED
George House, Units 12 & 13, Beevor Street, Off Pontefract Road,
Barnsley, South Yorkshire, S71 1HN, England
E-mail: enquiries@pen-and-sword.co.uk
Website: www.pen-and-sword.co.uk

or

PEN AND SWORD BOOKS
1950 Lawrence Rd, Havertown, PA 19083, USA
E-mail: uspen-and-sword@casematepublishers.com
Website: www.penandswordbooks.com

MIX
Paper | Supporting responsible forestry
FSC® C013604

Contents

Chapter 1

A strange reunion

Sunday 20 July 1997 was a warm and sunny day in Pau, a town in the Pyrenées Atlantiques *département* of south-west France which had been the capital of the ancient kingdom of Béarn. Quite early that morning a convoy of tourist coaches parked in one of the main streets began to fill up with middle-aged and elderly visitors who had spent the night in comfortable, but not luxurious, hotels. They were all members of an *Amicale.* The word means an association of people with a shared experience: women who were old girls of the same school, for example, or men who had served in the same branch of the military. The people clambering aboard these coaches belonged to the Amicale du Camp de Gurs; they were survivors of a *French* concentration camp where many prisoners had died during incarceration during the Second World War under the collaborationist régime of Marshal Philippe Pétain and his scheming prime minister Pierre Laval. The foundation of the Amicale had itself been a reaction to the insanity of people in several countries denying that the Holocaust had ever happened – this despite the wealth of photographs and films taken by the proud perpetrators as they murdered unarmed, innocent people with pistols, rifle butts, bullets from military firearms including machine guns and with canisters of Zyklon B poison gas.

This was not the first time the Amicale visitors had come to Pau. Then, they had arrived hungry and thirsty in filthy, stinking cattle trucks fouled with their own excrement, from which they had been chased by shouting and swearing gendarmes with loaded rifles and Alsatian dogs, hustling them onto crowded open lorries for the one-hour journey to Gurs. Adults of both sexes, some alone and some in couples, women with one or several children – even carrying babes in arms or pregnant and soon to give birth – they had all been treated the same, for they were categorised as *indésirables* in the country that had been la République Française and was re-named l'État Français after the defeat of 1940. The old revolutionary slogan *Liberté, Égalité, Fraternité* no longer existed, and the Declaration of the Rights of Man so proudly proclaimed there in 1789 was just a piece of torn-up paper. Some of the prisoners spoke French and had lived in France for decades before being deprived of all civic rights by Pétain and Laval, but thousands of them could not speak French and many did not even know in which country they were about to live, and maybe die, in a nightmare environment circumscribed by barbed wire. Among the prisoners emerging from the cattle trucks was a distraught 12-year-old girl from Berlin clinging tightly to her father's hand. Her mother had died and been buried, wrapped in a bed-sheet, at a different camp a few days earlier.

The prisoners saw nothing of the town. For them, it was just a way-station on the journey from one terrestrial hell to another, but as the coaches started their journey driving along the Boulevard des Pyrenées on that sunny morning of July 1997 the passengers saw to their amazement that Pau was an elegant town. Between the wars, it had been home to a community of British expats who enjoyed the mild climate and the brilliant light. Laure Schindler was a woman of seventy, a small and frail-looking 'old lady', as she termed herself, afflicted with the early stages of Parkinson's disease. She sat in the coach blinking at the sunlit beauty of the Pyrenees, their peaks still shrouded in snow, and wondered what the camp would look like after all the decades she had spent living in other countries before returning to France on her retirement.

She had been invited to this reunion by the *Fédération Nationale des Déportés, Internés Résistants et Patriotes* – the national association of former prisoners. After some hesitation, she accepted the invitation, thinking that perhaps freely to go back to Gurs and freely to leave it again was a way of exorcising some of the terrible memories of her time in the camp. Many of the returning former prisoners had attended a series of talks about the French concentration camps on the previous day, but she had not wanted to sit through long debates, however important and interesting they might be for others. She had come just for the commemorative ceremony on that sunny Sunday, thinking that, as her Parkinson's disease progressed, she might not have another chance.

After the 5½-hour train journey from Paris to Pau on the previous day, sitting in the coach on that sunny morning she had the impression of being on a tourist trip. The journey from Pau to Gurs took just over an hour, during which time she was aware of her heart beating faster and faster. On the road signs, she read *Gurs 7 km* and *Gurs 3 km* as she sat scanning the landscape, trying to catch a glimpse of the camp. The coach stopped in the middle of nowhere and people started getting out. Laure was among the last to do so. But where was the camp? she wondered. Where were the barbed-wire fences? Where were the huts? Where was all that knee-deep mud? Where the stinking latrines? Instead, the ground was covered in lush green grass. Few people now walked on it, so it had not reverted to the deep, clinging mud that had made the prisoners' lives so additionally miserable.

It was impossible even to see where the main gate of the camp had stood. She had never forgotten standing there as the lorry took away her father to his death in the transit camp at Noé. Never a strong person, he had leaned down as it departed to call out to her, '*Wir sehen uns bald wieder*', which was a lie, for they would never see each other again. And then, fainter still, his last words to her were, '*Haltung, Bummerl!*' The word *Haltung!* was a plea for her to hold on and not give up, and Bummerl was his pet-name for her, which no one else had ever used, and no one would ever utter again.

Her whole body racked with sobs, she had stared through her tears after him until the lorry was out of sight, for her *Vati* was the only relative she had left in the world. Still weeping, she ran back to her 'home' – a stretch of floor in one of the barracks with a smelly palliasse to sleep on and a single blanket. There she was found, still sobbing, by two adult sisters, Marthe and Elsie, who had 'adopted' Laure in the camp and stood in line each day to collect her scant rations, without which she would have starved to death, unable to compete with several thousand women intent on grabbing food for their own children. The two sisters lifted her to her feet and she heard them talking to her softly as they led her to the southern perimeter fence, to look beyond the wire at the fields and woods and the timeless mountains in the distance with their snow-capped peaks. It was a view that always calmed her. Eventually, she stopped sobbing, but the thin 12-year-old girl standing between her two camp-aunts knew the world would never be the same again.

The old lady visiting in 1997 wondered what she had been expecting. To see a skinny girl, then called Lore, with wide, terrified eyes staring at her elderly visitor? Surely not. She found a noticeboard recording the approximate numbers of the different categories of prisoners incarcerated at Gurs. First had come the women and children in the families of Spaniards who had fought and lost the civil war against the fascist troops of General Francisco Franco. There were half a million of them who crossed into France at the end of that war in February 1939. They had all ended in one of the concentration camps near the Spanish border because the all-male government of Edouard Daladier did not want them to settle in France as civilians. French women then had no right to vote.

Looking at the board, Laure wondered in which category of prisoners the girl called Lore had been counted. Was she one of the 12,860 Jews interned in May-June 1940? No, and she was not one of the 6,500 deported from Baden-Württemberg, a number that included her adoptive aunts Marthe and Elsie. Nor was she among the 12,000 Jews arrested in France by the Vichy government, because she had never been arrested. The list went on, but she had not officially existed in the camp, so none of the categories included her. In the bureaucracy of the Pétainist regime that governed France from 1940 to 1944, the thin, starving girl with terrified eyes did not exist because she had no identity documents.

Laure found a small wooden pavilion with a sign saying it had been the office of Elsbeth Kasser, the beautiful German-Swiss volunteer who handed out mugs of milk and pieces of cheese there to the hungry children. She had been known as 'the angel of Gurs'. The hut seemed so much smaller than Laure remembered. There was no trace of the infirmary where young Lore had spent many weeks being nursed back to a semblance of health several times by the prisoner-nurse they called Schwester Käte. The camp had been divided into wired-off blocks, some for the men and some for female prisoners, but the fences were long gone. There were the mountains, sunlit that day, but Laure could not distinguish 'her' mountain, looking at which, with Elsie and Marthe standing on either side, she had briefly felt remote from the noise, the bustle, the stench and the terror of the camp.

Gurs had been liberated by units of the local Resistance on 25 August 1945 and the surviving prisoners released. It was then used to imprison a total of 3,370 black marketeers and collaborators who had worked for the German occupation, plus a few hundred anti-Franco Spaniards and a small number of German PoWs. Almost all the evidence that the camp had ever been there was removed after Charles de Gaulle's government finally closed this place of national shame on 31 December 1945. The site was then cleared by burning down the rotten, vermin-infested barracks and auctioning off cheaply those in reasonable condition; most were bought by local farmers, taken to pieces and carted away as timber to be rebuilt as barns for livestock.

In the five-and-a-half decades since the girl called Lore had left the camp with her Romanian-born welfare worker Elisabeth, trees, planted by local schoolchildren, had grown up. There was a short stretch of railway line among the trees that Laure did not recall because it had only been laid when the camp was demolished, as a symbol of all the deportations to allegedly 'unknown destinations' where the deportees would be murdered in the gas chambers.

There was a simple visitor centre with some almost life-size blow-ups of photographs recording everyday activities in the camp: women washing clothes – their own and their childen's – without soap in the cold water of the outdoor ablutions area; ill-dressed, solemn-faced, thin and scruffy children staring at the camera. Seeing these, Laure wondered whatever she must have looked like then, to merit Elisabeth calling her 'the thinnest child in the camp'.

What had she been expecting? To meet a thin-faced, wide-eyed, desperate, starving, scabies-infected girl with her hair full of lice staring at an old lady? Where were the perpetual crowds of thousands of desperate people who, for better or worse, were part of the Gurs she had known? Laure had been hoping confusedly that there would remain some things she could remember but the only thing she recognised was the cemetery with its thousand-plus tombstones bearing names from all over Europe, where the ceremony was to take place. Of the various speeches by former prisoners, the one that touched her most was given by an elderly gentleman, who had been one of the deportees from Baden-Württemberg. An even older ex-prisoner described the camp in horrifying terms, as he had known it in the winter of 1940-41. This reassured her that none of her childhood memories was exaggerated. On the contrary. Other speakers emphasised the complicity of the Vichy government in handing over its prisoners to the Germans in 1942, knowing they would be murdered in the death camps.

However, what finally reduced Laure to tears on that sunny day in 1997 was not the speeches, moving as they were, nor the flags, nor the fine memorials – one for the Jews and another for the anti-Franco Spaniards who lay in the cemetery – nor even the cemetery itself with its rows of gravestones bearing unknown names, among which could have been those of her parents or her own. It was when a group of women in one corner of the cemetery began singing *le chant des déportés* – the song of the deported prisoners. It began,

> *Loin dans l'infini s'étendent des grands prés marécageux*
> *Où pas un seul oiseau ne chante dans les arbres secs et creux.*

That could have been a description of the ubiquitous mud of the camp, where no birds sang in the dead trees. The song ended,

> *Mais un jour dans notre vie, le printemps refleurira.*

Well, the 'swampy fields' of the song had literally been replaced by a reflowering in springtime. Laure wiped away her tears and joined the women singing, remembering the Gala of Gratitude in 1944 at the Salle Pleyel – the biggest concert hall in Paris – when she and the massed choirs of other 'hidden children', who had survived the German occupation, thanks to unknown people risking their own lives to care for them, had sung that song together for the capacity audience composed of those who had saved their young lives. It was far from the best song ever written, but it expressed what they had all been feeling and there was not a dry eye in the whole audience.

Around her, with no barbed wire, no huts, no starving prisoners and no sentries, the landscape was serene and calming. Only the cemetery remained, where the dead were said to rest in peace. With her head full of all these thoughts, Laure got back into the coach for the return journey to Pau, later writing:

> More than fifty years have passed. After this painful revisiting of my past, I feel liberated and happier. With my manuscript finished, I realised I should have written it long ago because, as Elie Wiesel told us at the Conference in New York, each of us is the 'last link in a chain', and once we are dead, there will be no more witnesses to tell what really happened. In a sense, I have come out of hiding after half a century. Obviously my account is not more terrible or more painful than so many others, but it is mine, in which I face up to the deaths of my parents in those awful places. At last I have recognised for the first time their courage and their faith in a possible future. So, I have found them again.

My book has been written by the child who still exists in me, as in everyone else. It was also written by that old woman of today, to account for the person who emerged from my terrible childhood – this particular 'link in the chain'. I had thought that I was without hatred and bitterness. Yet, as I worked through the account of my childhood, I felt waves of hatred and bitterness, and a terrible anger. Yet, the real purpose of this voyage into the past was to try and obliterate all my negative feelings, inasmuch as this is humanly possible.[1]

Chapter 2

Once upon a time

On a different occasion, Laure was invited to contribute to a collection of memoirs by former inmates of Gurs. She chose to write about her father, Harry Schindler. Like English surnames such as Baker and Smith, in German a *Schindler* is a man who covers a roof or façade of a house with thin slices of wet-resistant wood, so the word is cognate with the English word 'shingle'. It was Harry's fault that both her parents died in the camps, in which she also suffered so terribly. But this was not an accusation.

> Once upon a time – that's how fairy stories begin, whether they are happy or sad – anyway, once upon a time, long ago in another country there was a man called Harry. He lived in Germany, where he had known a normal childhood with his sister Lucie and his parents, just like all his schoolfriends. From very young, he had two passions: reading and drawing. I know few details of his life as a young man or of the history of his family because he never spoke much about them, apart from a few anecdotes about his father, who seems to have had a great sense of humour, which Harry had inherited and expressed in his drawings, especially the caricatures.
>
> Harry pursued his university studies in dental surgery at Heidelberg before settling in Berlin. A confirmed bachelor, he was nearly forty when he met a young woman with whom he fell head over heels in love. Grete was a pediatrician, at a time when female doctors were rare. They married in 1923 despite a twelve-year difference in their ages. Harry's dental practice was successful. After the wedding, he was happy. Before, he had lived through his impressive collection of books, but marriage to his wife,

whom he loved deeply, changed his life entirely. I forgot to mention that Harry was Jewish, although not observant, because this in the Twenties was unimportant in Germany.

Like many middle-class couples at the time, they took their honeymoon in Venice. After four years of marriage, in May 1927 a daughter was born to Grete and Harry. Although he still loved his wife, his books and drawings, he *adored* this little daughter, whom he named Lore, after Heinrich Heine's book *Die Lorelei.* Heine being known as Harry may be why Lore's father was given that non-German name. After becoming a parent, he discovered within himself an enormous capacity for love and tenderness for this child of his. He still liked to read books by the giants of German literature, to draw and to listen to the music of Haydn, Bach, Mozart and Beethoven – as he said, 'like all respectable Germans'. Since Dr Grete Schindler was a very busy woman, supervising their daughter's upbringing was most often Harry's concern.

Harry loved the tales of Oscar Wilde, which he read to Lore as bedtime stories until she was old enough to read for herself, especially *The Selfish Giant*, to which she listened again and again. He used it to calm his daughter down when she was upset by Grete's impatience after a long day caring for her patients. The Schindlers shared the large and comfortable family apartment with a live-in cook and the nanny, Anna, who looked after Lore until she was nine because Grete worked long hours, caring for her patients. Lore had a pet canary and a collection of thirty dolls, one of them a rag doll named Herta, without whom in the bed beside her she could not go to sleep. She also had a teddy bear, which was lost one day in the Tiergarten park, causing floods of tears. Like many single children, Lore was lonely at home and invented an imaginary sister, to play with her – and sometimes an imaginary brother.

Harry enjoyed reading and re-reading the works of Goethe and Schiller, the poetry of Heine, the dissertations of Kant and Schopenhauer, the novels of Thomas Mann and Stephan Zweig [who fled Austria in 1934, aghast at the rise of Nazism, at first to London and then to Brazil, where he committed suicide in 1942]. But Harry's greatest joy was his daughter, who adored him in return. It is curious that he named her after Heine's poem retelling the Lorelei legend because the Lorelei is a large rock jutting up in the middle of the Rhine, restricting the flow and causing rapids that hurl boats onto the submerged rocks at its foot. However, in the German legend which inspired Heine's poem, the Lorelei is a beautiful golden-haired maiden who lures incautious boatmen onto the rocks, where they drown. This is itself a version of the Greek legend of the half-bird, half-woman sirens Scylla and Charybdis whose singing was supposed to lure sailors to their deaths in the dangerous strait of Messina. Heine's poem was set to music by several composers, so perhaps it was that which spoke to Harry's German soul. Otherwise, why name your daughter after such a fatal, albeit legendary character?

None of this made Harry outstanding. He never did anything spectacular or heroic, nor contributed to any great achievement. People described him as so good that he was incapable of believing in the existence of evil, even when Nazism began to target him and his family. He believed in a civilised world and in the civilised values expressed by the great German writers in their books. He believed in his wife as a great healer. He believed that his daughter would grow up in the civilisation his literary heroes had known. But he was blind to evil and did not see that his country was falling into the darkest abyss, taking with it the wife he loved and the daughter he adored.[1]

At the age of five, Lore first overheard the adults talking about the Nazi party which came to power in 1933. One name occurred again and again: Adolf Hitler, leader of the *Nazionalsozialistischer Deutche Arbeiterpartei* (NSDAP). By birth, he was not German at all, but an Austrian-born citizen of the Austro-Hungarian Empire. To avoid deportation back to Austria, on 7 April 1925 he renounced his citizenship and became stateless. Nearly seven years later, he took German nationality on 25 February 1932 as a necessary step to achieving political office in the Weimar Republic under President Hindenburg. The Nazis holding the largest number of seats in the Reichstag, although not an absolute majority, Hitler was, as its leader, able a few months later to persuade Hindenburg to name him chancellor. Hindenburg's misgivings about the wisdom of this were mitigated by the appointment of former chancellor Franz von Papen as deputy chancellor, supposedly to keep Hitler under control.

In February 1933 he used the burning down of the Reichstag building by arson, which he blamed on the communists, to limit many liberties for all citizens of the Weimar Republic. After only three months in office, he had enacted a new law to 'reform the professional civil service', which included schoolteachers. All those defined as Jewish were sacked, as were similarly discriminated university teachers, including 25 per cent of Germany's Nobel prize-winners. In April 1933 German law disqualified Jewish doctors and surgeons from treating and operating on 'ethnic Germans'. The mayor of Munich forbade Jewish medical practitioners from treating any Gentile patients and the state of Bavaria denied Jewish students the right to attend medical school. Officially, if Grete and Harry continued to practise in Berlin, they had to restrict themselves to treating Jewish patients. Yet, as late as January 1933, the normally reliable *Frankfurter Zeitung* declared that it was 'a hopeless misjudgement to think that anyone could force a dictatorial regime upon the German nation because its majority calls for democracy'. On 31 January the national newspaper *Jüdischer Rundschau* wrote that 'within the German nation forces are active that would turn against a barbarian anti-Jewish policy'.

What did all this mean to a young girl, whose whole family was assimilated and considered itself completely German?

Lore having no problems in the classroom, school was a place for friendship and fun. She went skating with her classmates on an outdoor ice rink in winter and enjoyed excursions to swim in the Havel lake at the suburban beach in Wannsee during the summer term. That her parents were of Jewish origin, according to the Nazis' racial laws, formally introduced in November 1935, meant no more to Lore than that such and such a friend's family was from Saxony or Bavaria – until the dreadful day when her best friend Lieselotte refused to sit next to her in the classroom. Having been ordered to do this by her own mother, she would not even explain the reason for this rejection, causing Lore to run home in tears. Grete lied, saying that all the people currently being nasty to them would be sorry later 'when it was all over'. Unable to face up to unpleasant facts, Harry looked unhappy, but made no comment at all. Not long after Lieselotte's betrayal, the three Jewish girls in Lore's class were told by their teacher to leave the classroom and stand in the corridor outside during lessons which touched on the new National Socialist state and its Messiah, Adolf Hitler, which they were considered racially unfit to hear.

This produced in the three confused girls a vague and nameless feeling of shame as they tried to work out what they had done wrong. The next turn of the screw was for Jewish children to be expelled and forbidden admission to all German public schools. To continue their education, the previously sacked Jewish teachers improvised classrooms in spare rooms behind synagogues. In one of these, Lore was relieved to find herself welcome among other stigmatised girls – and boys, for the first time. There, she learned that some Jews had a language of their own called Hebrew and lived in a far-off country where oranges grew on trees. It all sounded rather fun to her, but adults did not think so, and some friends of her parents were already departing to live in other European countries or America.

In the state schools, the curriculum was completely changed by the Nazis, with 'intellectual' subjects reduced in importance and eventually banned in favour of several hours of physical activity for both sexes every day. All boys had to join the *Hitlerjugend* or Hitler Youth movement, with girls obliged to become members of the *Bund Deutscher Mädel* – the League of German Girls. Every child had to prove his or her family's loyalty by wearing their Hitlerjugend or BDM uniforms to school. Like other Jewish children, when Lore and her friends left their improvised school at the end of the afternoon, they were jeered at and jostled, for no reason they could understand, by older boys in Hitlerjugend uniforms. As neighbours and friends turned away in embarrassment and refused to even greet them, one person alone did not change. Had Anna, the 50-year-old nanny, been younger, it would have been illegal for her to be employed by the Schindlers. Post-menopausal German women could still work in Jewish households for a time, but Anna had been sacked by Grete so that she would not suffer the stigma of working for the Schindler family. Yet Anna insisted on coming regularly to visit them, making it plain what she thought of Hitler and the Nazis, despite Grete's warnings to keep her thoughts to herself elsewhere.

In that time, before modern transportation made long journeys on holiday possible, many Berliners holidayed in boarding houses among the woods around the lakes formed by the River Spree, only a few miles from their homes in the city. The prosperous Schindlers, however, enjoyed real seaside holidays on Germany's Baltic coast. The highlight of Lore's summer holidays was to be sent on a 200-mile train journey, in the care of the guard and bearing a label with her name and destination, to visit her maternal grandparents in what was then German Breslau and is now Wrocław in Poland. There her grandmother Oma and her unmarried aunt known as *Tante* Irma spoiled their young visitor even more than Lore's nanny Anna and her father did at home. Grandfather, called Opa, told her stories he made up especially for her, but kept at a distance because he was dying of tuberculosis, known to be highly contagious and then having no known cure.

The rest of the year in Berlin, weekends featured the Sunday visits to Lore's unmarried paternal great-aunts, Minka, who was a teacher of Italian, and Rosa, who looked after their house, which was filled with knick-knacks and precious possessions that Lore was always frightened of accidentally breaking. Sometimes the Sunday visit was to the home of the third sister, Malchen, and her husband Arthur, who was a lawyer. When Lore, then adult, tried to trace these relatives after the Second World War, they were all dead.

After her eighth birthday, her proudest possession was a wristwatch, something few German families could afford for a child at the time. When she was nearly nine Harry gave her a copy of Schiller's *Mary Stuart*, which caused his daughter to walk in tears around the apartment because she knew that unfortunate queen was going to have her head chopped off before the end of the book. Because well-to-do German families required their children to play a musical instrument, the only blemish on Lore's idyllic early years was the weekly visit of Frau Markoschewitz, her piano teacher, whose harsh Russian-accented voice nagged the spoiled daughter of the Schindlers to practise on the family's grand piano between lessons: '*Űben musst Du, Lore*! *Übe*!'

One day, Harry came home very upset. It was his habit in warm weather to take a book and read in one of the Berlin parks. On that day, he had sat down on a bench in a public garden, to read. It was a sunny day and the world seemed at peace. Then he noticed, written on the back of the bench *Juden verboten.* The bench was forbidden for Jews! He came home pale with worry after what must have been his first direct contact with the forces of Nazism which were taking over his country, but in which he had until then refused to believe. So, he deluded himself into believing that the writing on the bench was the work of some nasty child. There was a saying 'there's none so blind as them that won't see' and Harry was a prime example.

How he managed to delude himself in the face of the early measures enacted by the Hitler regime is due to his unwavering belief in the supremely civilised nature of the German nation. He was convinced that eventually Hitler, Göring, Goebbels and Himmler would be thrown out of power with their street-thugs, and life would go back to the good old days. Grete had no such illusions. She wanted to leave Germany while it was still possible, but he refused to listen to her, even when they were both forbidden to practise in Germany. The Law for the Restoration of the Professional Civil Service also expelled Jews from the civil service, which included teaching in schools and universities. By early 1934 the army had fired all its Jewish civilian employees; there was a *numerus clausus* of 1.5 per cent for Jews in schools and university; Jewish actors and actresses were not allowed on the stage or in films and Jews were no longer permitted to observe their dietary laws. They had to register all their possessions and wealth in Germany and abroad, for eventual expropriation by Nazi law at prices far below their market value. Worse was to come. The Nuremburg Race Laws that came into effect in September 1935 expelled Jewish officers from the armed services and forbade Jewish students who managed to study under the quota system from qualifying professionally.

Harry's persistence of belief in the intrinsic goodness of the German nation caused bitter arguments between Lore's parents, which deeply troubled their daughter. At last, in 1937, when Lore was nine, even Harry realised that his cloud-cuckoo vision of the world was a dangerous illusion. Neither he nor Grete could legally practise their professions in Germany, so there was no choice but emigration. However, thanks to his dithering, it was already too late. Visits by her parents to one consulate after another proved to Lore that most of the escape routes which had formerly been open to professionally qualified German émigrés were now closed. It was true that they could have obtained a visa for Paraguay, but that required a transit visa for Uruguay, which they could not have. Every possibility seemed to be cancelled by another impossibility. At last, thanks to a distant cousin in the USA, they were put on a waiting list for an American visa, but when Grete saw that list at the American consulate it was long and the three Schindlers' names were at the bottom.

Like many mild-mannered people, Harry was very stubborn and clung to his delusions, until the night of 11 November 1938, which became known as *Kristallnacht*.

Chapter 3

The night of broken glass

On 7 November 1938 a 29-year-old third secretary at the German Embassy in Paris named Ernst vom Rath was assassinated by 17-year-old Herschel Grynspan, using an automatic pistol, which he had purchased illegally that morning, to pump five bullets into his victim. Although he was standing close to vom Rath, only two bullets caused life-threatening wounds by hitting vom Rath's abdomen. Making no move to attempt to escape, the young assassin allowed himself to be arrested by French police after confessing to the shooting.

The previous month, the Nazi government had revoked all residence permits for foreign-born citizens. On 28 October some 12,000 people born in Poland, or descended from ancestors born there, were forcibly put on trains to the German-Polish frontier and warned that they would be shot if they tried to return home. Dumped at the border near the town of Zbąszyń with one small suitcase each and any German money in excess of 10 marks per person confiscated at the time of arrest, together with all their other property, they had another shock when the Polish frontier guards refused to let most of them enter the country because the Warsaw government had revoked the right of return for citizens who had been abroad more than five years. Thousands of these suddenly stateless persons were stranded at the frontier in increasingly harsh weather. Just 4,000 – who had been away for less than five years – were allowed to enter Poland. Two of the 8,000 unfortunates left behind at the frontier were Herschel Grynspan's parents, Zendel and Riva, who had been living in Hannover since 1911. Conditions on the frontier in the worsening autumn weather were so bad that some refugees tried to sneak back into Germany, despite the warning they had been given, and were shot by the German border guards.

Desperate, the Grynspans managed to send a postcard to their son Herschel, who was living illegally with an uncle in Paris. They pleaded for any money he could send them so that they could pay for food and shelter on the border. The card arrived in Paris on 3 November. What Herschel did between receiving it and shooting vom Rath we do not know. The world accepted that his act was a desperate reaction to what was happening on the Polish-German border, but there is another explanation.

Vom Rath died in a French hospital on 9 November. That evening, Hitler was celebrating the anniversary of the Beer Hall putsch in 1923 with his closest Party cronies. After he left the party early without delivering one of his habitual diatribes, Propaganda Minister Josef Goebbels made a speech which included instructions to Party members that, if spontaneous demonstrations of revenge on Jews for the murder of vom Rath erupted, they were not to be interfered with. In Nazi double-talk, this was as good as an order to take nationwide revenge on the whole Jewish community for the murder of the young diplomat in Paris. The inner circle of the Party disagreed. Even Göring and Himmler considered it unwise at that juncture, but Goebbels feared that his position in the leadership was slipping due to poor performance during the Sudeten crisis and wanted to make a show of strength. He also had another, more pressing, reason to attempt to regain favour in Hitler's eyes.

Had the casting couch not already long been in existence, Goebbels would have invented it. For two years, his position as German Propaganda Minister made him the *de facto* head of the German film industry with power to advance or ruin the careers of its stars. He had enjoyed numerous sexual liaisons with actresses seeking parts in his films and also had a longstanding affair with the beautiful Czech film star Lida Baarová, whom he wished to marry after divorcing his wife Magda. Hitler disapproved of this because he knew Magda and had been best man at her wedding to Goebbels. In the Nazi pantheon Herr and Frau Goebbels were portrayed as the perfect German couple. As if all that was not bad enough, Baarová was not German. Neither was Hitler, of course.

At 1.20 am on 10 November 1938 Reinhard Heydrich, the most powerful police official in Germany, sent urgent telegrams to all *Staatssicherheit* and *Polizei* offices and to SA leaders ordering them not to intervene in the revenge riots for the murder in Paris, except to protect foreigners and safeguard non-Jewish property that might be at risk. The night of unparalleled violence became known as Kristallnacht, or night of broken glass, when the pavements and streets of every German town centre were covered in shards after the display windows of 7,000 shops and twenty-nine department stores were smashed by the rioters. Thousands of Jewish homes, shops and synagogues were set ablaze with fire services taking no action, being present only to protect neighbouring German property, so fires in high street shops were doused, to save neighbouring shops, but fires in detached homes and synagogues were left alone. As dawn broke, flames still raged and acrid smoke drifted across town centres all across Germany.

Although it was generally accepted at the time internationally that the assassination of vom Rath was politically motivated, that did not explain why Herschel Grynspan had selected him as his target from all the other German diplomats in Paris because the unlucky secretary was openly anti-Nazi and already under investigation by the Gestapo for his 'political unreliability'. First imprisoned in Paris, then handed over to the Gestapo after the French defeat in the summer of 1940, Grynspan confessed after routine torture to having had another motive for the killing. Much later, the highly respected German historian Professor Hans-Jürgen Döscher[1] echoed Nobel Prize-winning French author André Gide's amazement at the time that no newspapers covered the true story. It was common knowledge in gay Paree at the time that Grynspan and vom Rath had first met at le Boeuf sur le Toit, an up-market restaurant and music hall, of which the *brasserie* was then a well-known homosexual rendezvous.

Whether the couple's affair had been motivated by lust or affection, perhaps with Grynspan killing his lover from jealousy when the affair was broken off, or whether he had consented to the affair in the hope that vom Rath could provide his parents with papers in a new identity, and then taken his revenge when that proved impossible, we simply do not know.

On the morning after Kristallnacht, when the streets of every German town were covered in shards of glass and filled with the acrid smoke from the burned synagogues and Jewish shops, Hermann Göring telephoned Goebbels to yell at him that it was senseless to destroy so much property which could have been taken over and used by the state. Instead of backing down, Goebbels planned to intensify *Aktion* Rath, as he called it, with local Gestapo offices all over Germany ordered to arrest 30,000 prosperous Jewish men and send them, with varying degrees of humiliation and ill treatment en route, to the concentration camps at Dachau and elsewhere which the Nazis had set up for 'internal enemies of the state' – a category that included Jews, homosexuals, communists and even Jehovah's Witnesses, whose beliefs prevented them swearing loyalty to the Nazi government. In addition, turning history on its head, the Jewish community was ordered to pay for all the damage caused in the night of terror and arson by the imposition of a collective fine of a billion marks,[2] allegedly to punish them for causing the riots.

On the morning after Kristallnacht, guarded by a strong police escort and surrounded by Nazi supporters jeering and singing the 'Horst Wessel Lied',[3] 6,000 men were arrested in Berlin and marched through the streets en route for the nearest concentration camp. Dr Harry Schindler was not at home when two Gestapo men came for him because he had been given temporary refuge in the home of a very courageous Gentile friend. Grete and Lore hid behind the curtains of their apartment as a mob of Nazis in the street below screamed abuse and sang the 'Horst Wessel Lied' about Jewish blood spurting from their knives. Mother and daughter were frightened that the mob might invade the building and break into their apartment.

Lore asked her mother, '*Warum, Mutti, warum*?' Why are they doing this? Pale-faced and rigid with terror. Grete replied, '*Ich weiss es nicht, Lore. Ich weiss es nicht.*' I just don't know, Lore.

Harry returned to the family's apartment in Charlottenburg the next day, however, fearing that his wife and daughter would suffer in his place if he remained in hiding. He was greeted by Grete embracing him for this show of courage. Later, this show of affection was one of Lore's happiest memories, contrasting with the anger and arguments between her parents that had made their home so unhappy since 1933. On the following morning, she clung to her father's arm when the two Gestapo men in trench-coats returned and politely asked to speak to Dr Schindler. Telling her gently to let go, he promised, '*Ich komme bald zurück.*' I'll soon be home again. While Grete packed a bag for him, Lore looked at the two men waiting in the hallway. Quietly spoken and neither tall nor blond, they seemed so different from the screaming mob of the previous day, more like clerks behind the counter of a bank. As the door closed behind the three men, Lore's childhood ended.

All over the civilised world, there was shock and outrage at what was happening in Germany. The Archbishop of Canterbury, Cosmo Gordon Lang, wrote a letter to the editor of the London *Times* on 12 November including the sentence, 'There are times when the mere instincts of humanity make silence impossible'. Thousands of Americans demonstrated at huge rallies held in support of the German Jews. At least one German ambassador reported to Berlin his fear that such protests might jeopardise the Western democracies' acceptance of Hitler's annexation of the Sudetenland area of Czechoslovakia. The British and French governments – still thinking that one could deal diplomatically with Hitler – pussyfooted around the issues. Members of the House of Commons requested Prime Minister Neville Chamberlain to condemn the pogrom. Still in Hitler's thrall, despite all the lies he had been told by the German chancellor, Chamberlain shuffled his papers and muttered in reply that the newspaper reports were substantially correct. He expressed deep sympathy for all the people suffering for what he termed 'the senseless crime committed in Paris'. In that city a newspaper editor who went into print protesting against what he termed 'the contemptible persecution of defenceless Jews and their wives and children' was warned not to cause waves.

In the USA politicians and clergymen of all denominations condemned the burning of synagogues and the violence against Jewish people. President Franklin D. Roosevelt started a press conference six days after Kristallnacht by stating that he could scarcely believe that such things could occur in a twentieth-century civilisation. He announced that Washington was withdrawing its ambassador in Berlin but made no practical gesture of help to the thousands of Jews still living in Hitler's expanded Reich, and who were now desperate to leave it. In the aftermath of the Great Depression, the traditional American isolationism, first formally expressed 110 years earlier in the Monroe Doctrine, was strengthened by a widespread fear of renewed unemployment. This led many Americans to accept the idea of a few famous Jewish writers, artists, and scientists coming to the USA, but they were not willing to let in thousands of ordinary refugees.

Even when a bill to admit 20,000 children at risk, their expenses paid by Jewish charities, was presented to Congress on the model of the British *Kindertransporte* that brought 10,000 Jewish children to the United Kingdom in 1938 and 1939, the wife of the US commissioner of immigration warned that these '20,000 charming children would all too soon grow into 20,000 ugly (i.e. job-hunting) adults'. In January 1939 a Gallup poll showed that 60 per cent of respondents were against the idea. The bill was not passed.

After Harry's arrest, Grete went several times to Gestapo headquarters in the PrinzAlbrechtstrasse, ignoring the perpetual insults of the staff as she sought news of his whereabouts. She traced him to the concentration camp at Sachsenhausen, a scant thirty-minute drive north of their home in Charlottenburg. Lore's ever-loyal nanny Anna baked a special cake for him, to cheer Harry up, and had to be persuaded by Grete not to take it to the concentration camp, in case there were 'consequences' for her.

Built into Goebbels' Aktion Rath was permission for relatives to visit the prisoners, not for humanitarian reasons, but precisely so that they could witness the appalling conditions and brutal regime in the camp. Seeing the effect of this on her traumatised husband, physically ill from the forced labour, the beatings and hours-long outdoor roll calls in deliberately inadequate clothing and the shattering of all his trust in the essential goodness of the German people, Grete had no need of her medical training to realise that he had not long to live under those conditions.

A further provision of Aktion Rath permitted relatives to pay high ransoms to obtain the release of their arrested menfolk. This Grete did, signing an undertaking for the whole family to leave Germany within two months after transferring ownership of all their wealth and property to the Nazi state. As Goebbels well knew, it was by this juncture virtually impossible to find another country which would accept Jewish refugees. When Harry arrived back at the apartment in Charlottenburg six long weeks after his arrest, his haggard appearance and shattered health shocked his 10-year-old daughter. Lore was even more alarmed when he went into his library, sobbing uncontrollably at the loss of all his illusions about the German nation, and destroyed, one after another, all the precious first-edition books he had treasured for years, stamping torn pages and damaged book bindings into the carpet in a paroxysm of hopeless anger and despair, before slumping down in his favourite chair until Grete persuaded him to go to bed.

For weeks he stayed there, being nursed back to a semblance of health by her. Another visit from the Gestapo warned her that the family's exit visas and passports would be cancelled if they had not left the country by the end of the month. Distraught, Grete realised that looking for safe storage for their furniture was a waste of time, since they would *never* be coming back to Germany. Lore's widowed grandmother and her unmarried daughter having acquired visas for Shanghai, one of the few places that would accept them, they paid a visit to Berlin, to say goodbye just before departing.[4] What became of her other relatives, who stayed in Germany, Lore was never told.

The most difficult moment for her was when her beloved nanny Anna came to bid her farewell.

To leave Germany before the end of the month, Grete – the respectable previously law-abiding doctor – was reduced in the last week to buying at an exorbitant price on the black market three temporary visas that entitled the family to live for one month in Belgium. They packed three small suitcases. In Lore's was her favourite rag doll Herta and a slim book of Heine's poems that had somehow escaped the destruction of Harry's other first editions. She did this in the hope that she could give it to him as a present when they arrived in Brussels, to jerk him out of the despondency in which he wallowed. A one-month stay in Brussels was only a temporary solution to their problems but, in such circumstances, people grasp at straws and it was rumoured that there was in the Belgian capital a committee which assisted refugees.

Grete also purchased the most expensive camera of the famous Leica range to smuggle out of Germany and sell for cash in some dire emergency. How she managed that was something Lore never learned. Had it been discovered at the frontier, this could have cost them their liberty, or even their lives. Allowed legally to take with them just one small suitcase and 10 marks each, the family changed trains at Cologne and stepped down from the second train at the Belgian frontier to be body-searched. For Grete and Lore, this meant stripping naked while a uniformed Gestapo woman went through all their clothing and footwear, then used her fingers to probe their mouths and other orifices in case they had concealed any jewellery there. Lore was terrified and on the edge of tears but took her cue from her mother's refusal to show any emotion throughout this humiliation.

The relief as the Belgian train chugged its way further and further from their previous lives was so profound that, for the first time ever, Lore saw her mother break down in tears. Instead of being alarmed, she found this strangely comforting because it showed that Grete, normally so remote and controlled, was human after all. Harry emerged from the torpor that had lasted since his return from Sachsenhausen, to propose a celebration dinner to mark their being free and all together! A part of their combined total budget of 30 marks was splurged on a meal in the dining car. For a brief moment, Harry seemed like his old self, joking, when they were served *Apfelstrudel* as dessert, that they had escaped from Hitler's Germany only to be eating their favourite Austrian dessert in a Belgian train. The euphoria dimmed somewhat on arrival in Brussels, to be replaced by an overpowering fatigue, with Grete and Harry unable to walk further from the station than the nearest cheap hotel, where Lore slept through the night on a single bed in their room with the doll Herta beside her. Her exhausted parents did not move until the next morning.

Chapter 4

Hitler breaks a promise

Belgium is a complicated country. In 1938 it was little more than a century old, having been created as a buffer-state to separate France and Germany after the Napoleonic wars. It was composed partly of formerly French territory and partly of German land. Even today, people in the north and east speak a low-German dialect called Flemish while the rest of the country speaks French. So, there are still tensions between the Flemings and the Walloons, as the French-speakers are known. Belgians never had a good press for their conduct during the Second World War, yet it is a little-known fact that, once a German invasion became imminent in the summer of 1939, the Belgian authorities changed the birth certificates of Jewish children, attributing them to parents with very Flemish or French names, which protected them from the ghastly fate that would otherwise have been theirs after the invasion that September.

Lore awoke on her first morning in Brussels, knowing nobody in this strange new world except her parents, and they seemed in a daze. Harry had always been a dreamer, leaving Grete to make decisions, but Lore now felt an unnamable anger at him for staying mentally locked in the obscenity of the concentration camp instead of attacking the reality of their lives as refugees. Even Grete seemed not to be her usual positive driving self. It was, however, she who pulled herself together, sought out the refugees' committee and acquired some funds from earlier German émigrés, who had arrived when it was still possible to bring out their capital. The funds were only enough, however, to afford limited food and a rented furnished room above a smoked-herring shop, which was cheap because it stank of rollmops. Even to Lore's youthful eyes, the unheated room was ugly, with old, unmatching furniture and a perpetual smell of fish.

Taking the book of poems from her small suitcase, she presented it to her father. Instead of the delight she had hoped for, he took it without reaction, saying politely, '*Danke, Bummerl. Das war eine gute Idee.*' That was a good idea? Once outside in the street, she found she could not understand a word of what people were saying to each other in French or Flemish. Putting on a brave face, Grete said nothing mattered so long as they were together and free. But the stress and anguish of the last weeks and the cold and damp conditions in the smelly, unheated room brought her down with a severe bronchitis that kept her in bed despite the urgent need to extend their visas, without which they would have been sent back to Germany. Harry having to step into the breach, he and Lore joined a long queue of refugees at Brussels' main *commissariat de police*. There, presumably because he looked so useless and forlorn and Lore was weeping uncontrollably, a well-dressed woman from the refugee committee named Martha Stern undertook all the negotiations with the Belgian authorities on their behalf. Becoming impatient with her father's silences, Lore told their saviour all the details she needed to negotiate a prolongation of several months of their residence permit.

Harry's pathetic inadequacy so concerned Martha Stern that she accompanied them back to the room above the herring shop, arranged for coal to be delivered so that the fire could be lit and also paid a Belgian doctor to call and prescribe medicine for Grete, who might otherwise have died in that time before antibiotics were available. Before the end of the day, it was agreed that Lore could go to stay with Madame Stern and her family in their villa on the outskirts of Brussels. The Sterns had left Germany just after Hitler's rise to power – as Grete had wished to do – and transferred their business to the Belgian capital without much financial loss. Immediately accepted by their son Kurt, aged 15 or 16, and their 13-year-old daughter, also called Lore, the new arrival loved every detail of their well-appointed villa, so like the comfortable bourgeois apartment in Charlottenburg where she had grown up. All the Stern family by now spoke fluent French, so Kurt undertook to give his new 'sister' daily lessons in the language, as a result of which she developed a terrible crush on him.

Returning to the herring shop after a few days, Lore found Grete gradually recovering. Although happy for her, Lore was guiltily aware that, when her mother was cured, her own life with the Sterns would come to an end and she would have to leave their happy home and return to her unhappy parents – a world of silences and recriminations. The fact that the Sterns told her she was always welcome in their home complicated the vortex of problems; a part of her wanted to stay with them and never go back to the cramped and smelly room above the herring shop, where all was despair, depression and arguments. It was a relief each day to go to school, where neither the staff nor the other pupils made her feel an outsider. The only unpleasant thing was having to go each morning to the headmistress' study – not for punishment but because she thought Lore was dangerously thin and sought to remedy this by daily doses of horrible-tasting cod liver oil.

When Grete had recovered her health, Martha Stern arranged with the refugees' committee for her to be appointed its doctor, looking after the many sick and malnourished refugees in Brussels in return for a small stipend that enabled the Schindlers to rent a two-room apartment in a nicer location. Treading a narrow line between what was legal or not under Belgian law, Grete examined other refugees and diagnosed their problems, referring severe cases to Belgian practitioners and dealing herself with routine injections and treatment of lesser ailments. Gradually, her morale went up, while Harry, who could not practise without all the equipment necessary for his profession, retreated yet further into another depression. At school Lore made friends of her own age among other refugee children, also unable to speak either of Belgium's official languages. In May 1939 she had her eleventh birthday. Unaware of the storm clouds gathering, she was sent to stay for several weeks with an old friend of her mother who had married a Dutchman named van Gelder and was living in Amsterdam with him. Placed in the care of two of Grete's patients for the journey, she was terrified when they were obliged to get off the train at the frontier, leaving her alone on the train, terrified because she was unable to speak to anyone or understand anything people said to her. However, once in Amsterdam with the van Gelders, life was fun, with trips to the zoo, boat trips along the canals and expeditions into the countryside. Dutch chocolate and cakes succeeded where castor oil had not and Lore began to put on some weight. She had no idea that this strange holiday arranged by her mother was a dream episode compared with what was shortly to happen.

On 13 May 1939 a luxury cruise liner of the Hamburg-Amerika line, the MS *Saint Louis*, had left the Belgian port of Antwerp, chartered by the American Joint Distribution Committee – known colloquially as 'the Joint' – to transport to freedom across the Atlantic more than 900 Jewish refugees who had signed all their property over to the Nazis in order to leave what had been their homeland. The equivalent of US $200-300 had been paid for each visa permitting one traveller to land in Cuba, from where the refugees hoped to make their way to the United States. On instructions from the very courageous captain Gustav Schröder, the obligatory portraits of Hitler all over the ship were taken down and ritual prayers were permitted in public spaces on board. The crew was instructed to treat all passengers with the normal courtesy due to peacetime passengers, the cinema and swimming pool were open and dances to the ship's orchestra were arranged each evening. It was all too good to be true.

It really was. On 27 May, as the ship moored off Havana, Cuban immigration officials came on board and most passengers' hopes were shattered. Twenty-two people with valid US visas were allowed to disembark, as were four Spanish citizens with valid papers. One other passenger who had attempted suicide was admitted to a Cuban hospital. Unknown to all the others remaining on board, the Cuban visas bought in Europe were invalid because Cuban president Federico Laredo Bru had cancelled all recently issued visas before the *Saint Louis* even set sail from Antwerp. Entry into the country now required a payment of $500 for each person and written permission from the secretaries of state and labour. Why? To their horror, the passengers were informed that the Cuban Director-General of Immigration, Manuel Benitez González, whose signature appeared on their papers, had amassed a personal fortune estimated at US $1 million by selling entry visas. When President Bru found out, he had forced González to resign and their precious visas were worthless.

The day after the *Saint Louis* moored off Havana, Lawrence Berenson, a Spanish-speaking attorney working for the Joint, flew to Cuba to negotiate with the Cuban president, convinced that he knew how to handle Latin-American politicians. On 2 June President Bru made an offer to him: to admit the passengers temporarily if the Joint posted a bond of $500 per passenger, making a total of US$ 453,000 plus 'other costs'. Berenson made a counter-offer of US$ 443,000, with no 'other costs'. He had misjudged his man. President Bru promptly ordered the ship out of Cuban territorial waters. With no option but to weigh anchor, Captain Schröder sailed to Florida, but the US authorities refused to allow the *Saint Louis* to dock at Miami, even after several direct requests had been cabled to President Franklin Roosevelt by the Joint and formerly important passengers on board. Canada also refused to accept the passengers, obliging Captain Schröder to sail back to Europe. Meantime, Morris Troper, European director of the Joint, which had chartered the ship, posted a bond worth US $8 million in modern values to cover the agreement by Britain, France, Belgium and Holland each to accept a limited number of the refugees: Britain took 287, France 224, Belgium 214 and Holland 181.

On 17 June the liner docked at Antwerp and the various quotas disembarked for asylum in Belgium and the other three countries granting asylum. Those who went to Britain were the luckiest; 254 of the others were swept up by the SS and Gestapo after German forces occupied the other countries. They perished in the extermination camps.[1]

Chapter 5

Trust the German soldier

After returning to Brussels, Lore met at school a Viennese girl of her own age named Marianne, who had been on the *Saint Louis*. The two girls became bosom pals, walking home together after school like any pair of sub-teenage girls, giggling at the funnier side of life in Brussels. Together they spoke German but tried to help each other learning French too. Once again, Lore felt guilty, preferring the warm and caring atmosphere of Marianne's home to the tensions of her own, with Harry silently staring into space and occasionally rousing himself to argue with Grete. After the war, Lore tried to trace the van Gelders, the Stern family and the mother of Marianne, her best friend in Brussels, but they had all apparently been murdered in one of Himmler's extermination camps.

Even Grete had not foreseen the speed at which the uneasy peace of 1938 would turn to a world war in 1939. Open warfare began on 1 September 1939 when the massed Germany army and Luftwaffe crossed the Polish frontier, allegedly responding to an attack on the Nazi radio station at Gleiwitz, which had been staged using concentration camp prisoners wearing Polish uniforms, whose slaughtered bodies were left there as 'evidence' of Polish aggression.

On 3 September Britain and France declared war on Germany. If the refugee children in Belgium innocently took this as grounds to plan their return home across the Rhine, their parents wondered nervously how long Belgian neutrality would be respected by Hitler. Lore was old enough to understand what the grown-ups were talking about sufficiently to dread the future. The 'phoney war' lasted until 10 May 1940 and was jokingly called *Sitzkrieg* by the Germans in contrast with the *Blitzkrieg* or lightning war that had torn its way through the western half of Poland, the eastern half being occupied by Soviet forces, as agreed in the secret protocol of the Ribbentrop-Molotov pact. Hitler had promised in 1937 to respect Belgian neutrality but, to him, as to Stalin, treaties and promises were just sheets of paper to confuse and wrongfoot his victims and then be torn up when it suited him.

This was the start of *Fall Gelb*, the invasion of Luxemburg, the Netherlands and Belgium. In theory, the German land forces' way to Brussels was blocked by a series of forts around the city of Liège and the biggest fortress in Europe at Eben-Emael, farther north. A giant construction of reinforced concrete set into the native rock of a hill overlooking the Albert Canal, with retractable observation and long-distance artillery cupolas let into its vast concrete roof, the fortress was thought to be impregnable. When Hitler, who at this early stage of the war did have some good ideas, was looking at an aerial view of the flat roof, even with a magnifying glass he could see no signs of either mines or obstacles on it. The reason was that it had been kept like that because the men cooped up inside the fortress sometimes used it to play football. Hitler summoned Lieutenant General Kurt Student, commanding 7th Flieger-Division. The two men discussed making a drop of paratroops onto the roof of the fortress, but Student pointed out that, even if the Luftwaffe's noisy and slow-flying Junkers Ju 52 transport aircraft managed to reach the fortress without being shot down, the best landing conditions would see each stick of men distributed over 300 yards. If it was a windy day, many of the paras would not even land on the roof but be blown sideways to land on the ground around the fortress.

To solve that problem, it was decided to transport the paras in gliders. Twelve of Student's DFS 230 gliders could land on the roof, disgorging a total of eighty or more men with their personal weapons *and* a mass of 50-kilogram hollow charges to insert into ventilation slits and gun cupolas to kill many of the men inside the fortress and put the gun lifts out of order, rendering the guns useless.

At 0330 hours on 10 May 1940 eleven Ju 52 aircraft took off from Cologne-Ostheim airport, each towing a DFS 230 glider to a height of over 8,000 feet. One glider's tow rope snapped on take-off. A second had to land short of Belgian territory. The other nine dropped their tow ropes at the frontier, the gliders continuing their way silently to the target. At 0415 a Belgian officer outside the fortress looked up and saw the nine gliders circling above his head, preparatory to landing. It was too late for the garrison to prevent them landing. On the roof of the fortress, within minutes the paras were already using their powerful charges of explosives to cripple the guns and kill the crews. Five minutes later, German ground forces crossed the Dutch and Belgian frontiers. The invasion was going like clockwork. In Brussels, Lore awoke at 0500 to a sunny spring morning marred by the sound of German bombs exploding nearby. It was the day before her twelfth birthday.

In Britain, the police rounded up all male German and Austrian refugees and shipped them off with fascists of all colours to confinement on the Isle of Man, a vast concentration camp that became known as 'the island of barbed wire'. In Belgium, similarly, the term 'enemy aliens' included foreign men of all political hues. So, at 11 o'clock that morning, Harry was arrested by two Belgian policemen on the first leg of a journey to an unknown destination. Watching this repeat of the arrest by the Gestapo eighteen months earlier, Lore saw her mother betraying no emotion, and wondered whether she was too shocked to say anything. This time Lore did not cling to Harry, not just because she was a little older but because he had, in a sense, left her long ago. She was nevertheless terrified by the way her father was suddenly torn from her universe, for reasons she could not comprehend.

Through the refugees' grapevine the wives of the arrested men learned that they had been taken to a barracks on the outskirts of Brussels, used as a holding camp where they were to be detained for a few days before being despatched elsewhere. Lore spent her birthday outside the barracks in a crowd of women and children hoping for news of their menfolk. Also in the crowd were Marianne and her mother. The only show of humanity was when the sirens sounded to warn of another incoming raid by the Luftwaffe and the guards allowed the waiting women and children to take shelter inside the walls until it was over. The next day passed in the same fashion. On the third day, the doors of the barracks opened for a column of prisoners to emerge, surrounded by guards with fixed bayonets, yelling at them to move faster. In all the noise and confusion, Harry stumbled past, looking like a man already dead and hardly glancing at his wife and daughter, even when Lore called out, '*Vati! Vati!*' Daddy, Daddy! An older girl whom Lore knew from school also called out to her father and tried to give him a small package of food for the journey, only to be knocked down with a sideways swipe of a Belgian bayonet, leaving her weeping on the ground, her small gift lying in the dust beside her as the column of despairing men continued on their way to the railway station. The women and children were prevented from following by a cordon of Belgian police.

Not even Martha Stern could trace what had become of Harry and the other arrested men. If no adult could understand what was happening, it was even more confusing for their children. Instead of writing her father off, as she had been doing after losing all respect for him, Lore now blamed herself for not showing him more affection and maybe giving him the strength to be the father he had been. Hearing that the German ground forces were still advancing, preceded by the Luftwaffe's daily dive-bombing raids – this was how the *Blitzkrieg* worked – Grete was torn between the idea of fleeing the approaching Wehrmacht and staying put so that any news from Harry could reach her. The latter decision was influenced by the fact that Belgium was theoretically protected by three French armies in the country, plus the small and ineffective British Expeditionary Force under General Lord Gort.

At this time conscripts across the border in France were being issued, not with rifles but picks and spades, which they were supposed to dig trenches and construct an extension of the Maginot Line It had been designed to stop short at the Belgian border on the assumption that the Germans would not be so ungentlemanly as to invade France by driving and marching around the end of the Line and coming through Belgium, supposedly protected by Hitler's promise not to do that, given two years before. Even in the critical sector of the line at Verdun, where over a million men had died in the battles of the First World War, there was not a single gun capable of stopping a Panzer.

Since the Belgian, French and British forces seemed unable to stop or even slow down the German invasion, Grete finally chose to flee with Lore into what she thought would be a safer haven in France, which had the largest army in Europe and was protected by the reputedly impenetrable fortifications of the Maginot Line. After mother and daughter had been waiting for a whole day sitting on bare concrete at the main Brussels station in a crowd of Belgians and foreign refugees fleeing the German advance, they grabbed their few belongings and raced to a platform where a train was scheduled to leave for the frontier. Dragging Lore by the hand, so as not to lose her in the mêlée, Grete fought her way through the throng to secure a single seat she could share with her. The train started to move and slowly gathered speed. Stopping and starting at frequent intervals, it finally arrived at a station where the name plaques had all been removed to confuse the enemy. Like all the refugees on board, Lore was confused and frightened that the train had not reached the border. There followed a terrifying night with several air raids that fortunately left the train unharmed until the station loudspeakers announced that it was returning to Brussels. The passengers were told by the train crew that America had entered the war, which would soon end in an Allied victory. It was obviously pure fabrication with no basis in fact, but such was the need to believe it that it triggered a festive atmosphere on the train with some passengers sharing their scant provisions with total strangers.

Back in Brussels, reality sank in with the news that Belgium was surrendering on 28 June after what its government called 'the eighteen-day war'. With the cessation of hostilities, it was obvious that the Wehrmacht would occupy Brussels in a few days. Their landlady refused to let Grete and Lore back into their apartment because there was a rumour that the Germans would punish anyone who gave shelter to a refugee. They were saved from spending the night on the streets by a woman with a Belgian Red Cross armband, one of a team that collected refugees and took them to an empty royal palace, where mattresses had been laid on the floor of the ballroom with a blanket apiece, and some food was available. Unable to sleep, Lore stared up at the crystal chandeliers above her head and contrasted their elegance with the human misery lying on the floor.

King Leopold III was not at the other royal palace when the Belgian flag was hauled down there and replaced by a swastika flag. Although the government had fled to Britain, the king had remained at his post as commander-in-chief of Belgian forces and was placed under house arrest by the new masters of his country. Despite Grete's promise that the German army was not the Gestapo, Lore was again terrified that she would be separated from her mother and confined in a concentration camp like the one at Sachsenhausen. She clung to the assurances of the Red Cross ladies that their palace was in an international zone, which the Germans would not be allowed to enter. So much for their trust in the rule of law! Two days later, terrified like everyone else there, Lore watched the first Nazi troops march into Brussels to the sound of thousands of hobnailed boots on the cobbled streets. Continental armies often sang on the march because they traditionally had to cover long distances on foot to arrive at the so-called field of honour, whereas the British soldier usually departed for the battle on board a ship. That these Wehrmacht men did not sing their marching songs was somehow all the more menacing. That morning the refugees also watched the Belgian flag being hauled down on the king's palace, yielding its flagstaff to the swastika flag, which they had hoped never to see again.

On the fifth day in their temporary haven, the refugees were expelled from the empty palace when the Wehrmacht simply overruled the Red Cross and drove everyone out at bayonet point. Grete was terrified because their temporary papers clearly showed that they were refugees from Germany. Although nobody then could have imagined the extermination camps like Auschwitz, the thought of being separated from her mother and locked up in a German concentration camp, as Harry had been, was frightening enough for Lore. Try, as she did, to explain to Lore that the soldiers in the streets were not the Gestapo, Grete was unable to lessen Lore's fear of any man in a German uniform. Returning to their apartment, she and Grete were allowed by the landlady to re-possess their rooms; she even deferred payment of the rent as a form of apology for her earlier behaviour, based on one unsubstantiated rumour among many.

At first, after the Belgian surrender, the German soldiery in Brussels was on its best behaviour, smiling, polite and even handing out sweets to children in the streets. Large posters everywhere depicted a strong and smiling German soldier holding a young girl by the hand and carrying a smaller boy on his other arm. In French and Flemish, the slogan read 'Abandoned populations, put your trust in the German soldier!' Millions of these posters had been printed in all the languages of Europe. Although she was still terrified when she heard Germans soldiers speaking her mother tongue in the streets, Lore gradually came to realise that they ignored children when checking adults' identity documents. With the German arrival in Brussels, the refugees' committee had been wound up. To earn a pittance with which to buy food, Grete re-started her illegal medical career, looking after other refugees. Lore returned to school and life in Brussels seemed, although difficult, not too dangerous.

Grete was at the time 42-years old – an age at which European women of today still look young – but for the past seven years, she had been coping with the unpleasantnesses and dangers of life in Hitler's Germany, her face looking increasingly worried and tense. Lore wondered whether she had ever been happy. In later life, when herself was an adult, Lore frequently wondered whether she would have understood Grete better if she had not died so young. Had the daughter inherited some characteristics from the mother, other than her slight physical build and a facial resemblance? It was impossible to know.

On 22 June France signed the Armistice in the same railway carriage where Germany had capitulated at the end of the First World War, parked in a clearing in the forest near Compiègne. This agreement sentenced its soldiers who had been taken prisoner to four years and more in German PoW camps. Hitler decided not to occupy and garrison the whole of France because that would require the immobilisation of hundreds of thousands of his soldiers, whom he would need for the invasion of the USSR he was planning in defiance of the non-aggression treaty signed by his foreign Minister Joachim von Ribbentrop and his Soviet counterpart Vyacheslav Molotov. France's two border provinces of Alsace and Lorraine were annexed into the Reich and the industrial north-east of France, plus a strip of varying width along the strategically important Channel and Atlantic coasts was physically occupied under military law by German troops. The other half of the country was the so-called Free Zone controlled by the collaborationist Marshal Philippe Pétain. With Paris in the occupied northern zone, Pétain's capital was in central France, at the spa town of Vichy. He changed the title of the country from République Française to État Français – from a republic to an undefined state – and replaced Robespierre's revolutionary slogan *liberté, égalité, fraternité* with *travail, famille, patrie*. Historian Simon Winder summed it up like this:

> [The Vichy government's decision] was meant to represent a victory for common sense, sharing with Britain a realistic end to the war, which was judged inevitable after such a total defeat. Its officials ranted about France's military failure being the result of 'the nation's pacifist schoolteachers', who were accused of destroying young men's instinct to fight for their country. When the war in fact carried on, Vichy was suddenly left as an embarrassment to itself, clung to by exhausted and demoralised French citizens, but without the panoply of Catholic quietism it had been intended to embody:

> merely collaborationist rather than realistic. Vichy printed banknotes with the compelling slogan *Industrial labour and farm labour: the two breasts of the republic* [ignoring Pétain's change of the name from 'Republic' to 'State'] and experimented with the classicist idea that Pétain's France would be Ceres [the Roman goddess of agriculture, harvests and fertility] to Germany's Vulcan [the Roman god of fire and metalworking]. It never stabilised but perhaps marginally shielded some of its citizens sometimes from the horrors of the new Empire [whose capital was Berlin].[1]

At the time of the Armistice, France was a country where women could not have a bank account, borrow money, vote or stand for office. Yet, in the highest strata of society, they controlled many of the top politicians traditionally, in the bedroom. The mistress of the last prime minister Paul Reynaud was la comtesse de Portes, described best as 'a middle-aged woman, with a shrill voice and a clamorous, demanding manner, who chattered like a magpie and lost her temper with ease.' When Reynaud was asked why he always did her bidding, he replied, 'A man will do anything for some peace at home after a hard day in politics.' After the capitulation, Renaud and the countess were fleeing the country with a fortune in gold and jewellery when he crashed his car driving far too fast. With no seat belts in those days, he nearly decapitated her and suffered severe head injuries himself. They had set off from their last stop, for lunch in a restaurant, in the throes of a violent argument, the continuation of which seems to have been the reason why he lost control of the car shortly afterwards.

Another powerful woman was the marquise de Crussol, the social-climbing daughter of a sardine millionaire, who ran the most important political and literary *salon* in Paris in the Thirties and was the mistress of Edouard Daladier, the previous PM. The two women detested each other, but they had nevertheless got together to arrange the transfer of power to Renaud, with no one else consulted. André Tardieu, founder of the Republican Centre party, was bedding Comédie Française star Mary Marquet. In that same theatre Popular Front Foreign Minister Yvan Delbos found his stately brunette mistress Germaine Rouer. There, too, Georges Mandel, *chef de cabinet* to Clemenceau, fell in love with the blonde, buxom actress Béatrice Betty. While French delegate to the League of Nations, Paul Boncour wrote to his mistress Magda Fontanges, 'When I think of your lovely body, I don't give a damn about Central Europe.' Embarrassingly, the letter was read out in court when the lady with the lovely body was on trial for shooting another lover, Count Charles Chambrun. To mis-quote the song, it was not money that made this world go round, but the terrible twins, sex and infidelity.

Chapter 6

News of Harry

In the weeks after the Germans marched into Brussels there was no financial help from the refugees' committee, which had been wound up. Somehow, Grete re-established her illicit medical practice for whatever small payments other refugees could afford. It was just enough to pay the rent and buy food for Lore, keeping little for herself. Grete was greatly relieved when a censored postcard arrived from Harry, on which several pre-printed messages had been scored through, leaving just the news that he was enjoying good health in a *French* concentration camp at Rivesaltes, on the Mediterranean coast between Perpignan and the Spanish frontier. Although still in what today would be the prime of life, Grete suffered from what was then called 'a weak chest', and her recurrent bronchitis flared up again with all the stress. Having given most of her food to Laure since arriving in Belgium, she was also suffering from malnutrition. However, their failure to reach France by train was doubly justified when an unkempt but resourceful escaper from the concentration camp at Rivesaltes knocked on the door at the end of September and told them that Harry was actually very ill there and suffering what sounded like a nervous breakdown.

Desperate to do something, Grete hatched what seemed, even to her 12-year-old daughter, a crazy plan. Only many years later did she appreciate the courage it must have required. Between May and the beginning of October 1940 the men in Wehrmacht uniforms on the streets of Brussels caused no problems for the refugees. There was no hint of the terror to come after the Gestapo and Allgemeine-SS installed themselves all over the country. Grete reasoned that, if that man could escape, using his own wits and with no other help, from a camp in southern France and make it all the way back to Brussels, then surely she could manage to get to the camp and persuade Harry to come back to Brussels, where at least she could care for him. To do that meant somehow crossing the militarised Belgian-French frontier and the heavily patrolled demarcation line between German-occupied France and the so-called Free Zone, in which Rivesaltes lay. There were plenty of people-smugglers offering to help refugees across the frontiers, but sadly many of them took their victims' money and disappeared with it; some even less principled handed their anguished clients over to the frontier guards for payment. Displaying the same shrewd intelligence that had got the family out of Germany, Grete found a wastepaper dealer who regularly smuggled people across the borders in the back of his lorry, hidden under bales of paper. His price was high but, thinking this to be their ultimate emergency, Grete sold their only possession of value – the Leica camera – to pay for him to drive her all the way to Perpignan in southern France and bring her back with Harry.

Grete wanted to leave Lore behind with some other German refugees in the comparative safety of Belgium, but this triggered a storm of hysterical protest: Lore refused to be abandoned by her mother as well as her father and left behind in Brussels with strangers. She made a terrible scene, weeping and screaming. When, finally, Grete seemed to be reconsidering her decision, Lore promised to behave like an adult and not cause any problems on the journey. Taking the little food they could acquire in the emergency conditions of occupied Brussels, one night both mother and daughter climbed into the rear of the wastepaper lorry parked in a dark side street and were then concealed behind and under the bales of paper by a man introduced anonymously as 'my colleague' by the driver, to whom Grete had paid half of the agreed fare; the remainder was to be handed over on the return journey.

The subterfuge succeeded in getting them across the French frontier to Paris, where they arrived before dawn, to pass the day in a grimy, no-questions-asked backstreet hotel habitually used by the people-smugglers for themselves and their clients who had no identity papers. It was customary at the time – and for many years after the end of the war – for guests to hand over their passports when arriving at a French hotel. At some time in the night a police officer in towns, or a gendarme if the hotel was in the countryside, would arrive and note the details of all the passports of that night's guests. These were telephoned to Paris, so that the Sûreté Nationale could compile a list each day of all the aliens who had stayed the night in hotels throughout France, and thus keep track of their movements.

Crossing the demarcation line between the occupied zone and the Free Zone was more onerous than crossing the Belgian-French frontier had been. The lorry halted in a forest a few miles from the line, guarded on the German side by armed soldiers and on the other side by men, also armed, of Pétain's *Armée de l'Occupation.* The paper merchant asked whether Grete and Lore could face a walk of two hours through the forest to avoid both sets of guards. Although visibly ill by then, Grete said she could manage that. They descended with the nameless 'colleague' while his boss drove on, to cross at an official access point, where the cargo was checked with bayonets poked into every bale and the spaces between. In the dark and gloomy forest, Lore was afraid of being stopped at gunpoint by a gendarme or German soldier lying in wait, and constantly worried by Grete's state of exhaustion. She was obviously finding it hard to walk at all. The guide had his work cut out helping her along the forest trails and at the same time trying to reassure Lore that all was well, despite having no common language. Having grown up in a town and knowing nothing about the countryside, she was terrified of the dark and alarmed by every noise made by an animal she could not see in the bushes around them. Even the hooting of an owl seemed threatening. After two hours' painful progress, they rendezvoused with the lorry on the other side of the line and, a few hours later, arrived at a small country inn, where they stayed the day. It was hardly luxury but a great deal more comfortable than the doss house in Paris.

The division of France after the capitulation

By the time they reached Perpignan after three days in the back of the lorry, Grete's bronchitis was much worse. After introducing them to the manager of a dirty, depressing backstreet hotel, similar to the one in Paris, the paper merchant promised to return in two weeks' time to drive them back to Brussels, and then drove off to deliver the load of paper to his client. They spent three days of terrible weather in Perpignan. To shelter from rainstorms during the day, they frequented a cheap café, where other refugees without papers sat for hours over one cup of coffee in almost silent gloom, occasionally hatching crazy and impractical plans. Grete went from table to table, quizzing the German-speakers among them about the best way to get Harry out of the camp. One of these men who stayed in Lore's memory was a thin, dark, bearded fellow who tried to dissuade Harry's obviously sick and exhausted wife from any hope of rescuing him, telling her of a recent escape attempt that ended with the prisoner caught, dragged back to the camp, beaten and placed in solitary confinement. An added complication was that the camp at Rivesaltes had been flooded by all the rain, which overwhelmed the inadequate sanitation system, causing faecal matter to float to the surface and even drowning several people. As a result, all the surviving prisoners had been transported in army lorries to another camp at nearby St Cyprien.

Lore thought at the time that the dark, bearded man was hostile, but later came to think that maybe he was giving her mother good advice. The three days spent in Perpignan were for Lore a nightmare. She was totally unaware of the elegant Mediterranean seaside town with its promenade and palm trees, the smart cafes and affluent tourists on the glassed-in pavement terraces drinking apéritifs who shut their eyes to the reality of the French defeat. Her entire world shrank down to the palpable hopelessness of the men in the café, some hoping against hope that they could escape to Spain by walking over the high Pyrenees, others just hoping not to be arrested that day as illegal immigrants. There seemed to be no women or children in the world; just these hopeless men. And Grete, who had always seemed so strong and capable, grew daily less and less in control of herself, never mind the hostile world in which they were adrift. At moments her confused and unhappy daughter hoped that, after all this advice, Grete was actually thinking of giving up what had always been an extremely ambitious plan, costing them their only possession of value, and travelling instead back to Brussels in the paper lorry without even visiting Harry in the concentration camp.

Twenty miles from Perpignan, the camp at St Cyprien had been built by the French government in the First World War and then re-opened to intern members of the defeated Republican forces and their families who managed to escape Spain at the end of its civil war in 1939. These had been turfed out to make room for the refugees from Belgium and other foreigners with no papers who had been rounded up in France. Watching her mother, increasingly desperate and feverish, Lore wondered what would happen if they did reach St Cyprien. Would the guards arrest them too? Anything seemed possible in her troubled imagination. They eventually took a country bus, which went around the villages before finally arriving at its terminus by the camp gate, where they stepped down into a world of barbed wire, drab uniform huts and armed guards.

It seemed briefly that Grete's plan might just work when she managed to persuade the guards to allow her to meet Harry. Under escort, they walked along the main street of the camp. Lore was shocked anew when the prisoner summoned to meet them was an old man, demoralised and skeletal, gaunt through semi-starvation and suffering what was thought to be dysentery. Was this really Harry, the *lieber Vati* she had so loved and who had read to her from his favourite books at home in Charlottenburg?

Hanna Schramm was a German-Jewish remedial teacher, sacked under the Nazi legislation of 1935, who moved to Paris, earning a precarious living as a teacher and journalist there and in Besançon. Arrested there, she was 46 years old when first incarcerated, and wrote after the war of life in the French concentration camps, telling how everyone was ill:

> The illness began with a high fever and terrible bloody diarrhoea with stomach cramps. The onset was so rapid that those affected soiled their clothing, their bedding and the floor before they had even realised they were ill. Some also had nausea, with their mucous membranes drying up, giving them intense thirst. They fainted and fell down, doubly incontinent.[1]

After the analysis of prisoners' faeces at St Cyprien in a military laboratory, a total lack of dysentery bacteria was announced. In the absence of a clear explanation of their condition, prisoners' rumours focused on typhoid fever caused by polluted drinking water. The rumour was immediately denied by the authorities, claiming that the situation in the camp was no worse than in neighbouring villages suffering outbreaks of gastro-enteritis. In the absence of any appropriate medicines, the sick prisoners were given herbal remedies without any effect. Letters from prisoners that got past the censors by one means or another described the 'ambulances' which took the sick to hospital as the same trucks that daily drove the previous night's corpses to the camp cemetery.[2]

When she saw Harry in the camp at St Cyprien, instead of embracing him, all Lore could do, was turn her face away and weep. With the natural self-centredness of her age, she was already wishing she had stayed in Brussels and let her mother be smuggled alone in the lorry all the way to the south of France. It was also impossible not to be aware that Grete was near the end of her strength. Lore was terrified of her sick mother having to go into hospital, leaving her alone in a country where she could not speak the language and had neither money nor identity papers. When Grete had finished explaining to Harry her impossible plan, which involved all three of them returning to Brussels in the wastepaper lorry on its next trip, Lore heard Harry say behind her back, '*Grete, lass mich zu Ruhe. Ich bin nicht fähig das anzuhören. Ich bin doch zu krank und zu schwach und Ihr sollten nicht hier gekommen sein.*' Leave me alone. I cannot even listen to you. I am too ill and too weak. You should not have come here.

They followed Harry back into his barrack, where the cotton palliasses – mattress covers stuffed with dried grass – were laid directly on the sand. He continued grumbling all the while about the hunger, the dysentery, the brutality of the guards and the torture of the sandflies that attacked the prisoners in the day and made sleep impossible at night. Lore was seized by a terrible anger as Harry poured out all his griefs and took no account of what his wife and child had suffered in coming all these hundreds of miles in terrible conditions and real danger, just to be with him. At the same time, she hated her mother for coming to bully Harry instead of leaving him in peace – or what passed for peace in this terrible place. Needing to blame somebody in order to account for her own misery, Lore blamed them both equally: Grete for obstinately pursuing her dream of saving Harry and him for not being the man of action he never had been, instead trying to make his wife understand that there was no way out of the impossible situation in which they found him. At the time all Lore could think was that neither of them was paying any attention to their anguished child.

Neither she nor they, of course, had at the time any way of knowing that, if Harry had agreed to come back with his wife and daughter to Belgium, they would all three have eventually been rounded up and transported hundreds of miles eastwards in cattle trucks to meet their deaths in a gas chamber. To add to all Lore's other miseries, the poor food and unhygienic life of the last few months had caused a hideous rash all over her body that itched and bled when she could not resist scratching it.

All Grete managed was to persuade the St Cyprien camp commandant to allow Harry to go out with his wife and daughter for a picnic in a field, after which he insisted on returning to the camp. Their money nearly exhausted, apart from the amount Grete was keeping for the return journey, she moved from the cheapest hotel in Perpignan to an even cheaper one in the little village of Elne, where tourists came to admire the beautiful medieval cloister, not that she and her increasingly distraught daughter were interested in architecture. They must have presented a sad sight to the locals, a sick and distraught foreign woman and her confused and unhappy daughter killing time each day by wandering through the two miles of countryside that separated Elne from the camp at St Cyprien. Fortunately, the October weather was warm, so near the Mediterranean.

On the last visit to Harry at the camp, Grete informed him that she had deliberately missed the departure of the lorry returning to Brussels and would wait near the camp in the hope of changing his mind and catching the lorry on its next fortnightly departure. Harry shrugged off this new gesture of affection and concern. Watching wide-eyed as her parents argued, Lore could see that he was wishing them just to go away and leave him alone. Through her tears, she watched her parents' last argument, neither of them paying her any notice. The dispute ended with her frail and very sick mother eventually collapsing unconscious. Carried into the camp by two guards, Grete was allowed to spend the night with Harry in an empty barrack block. A blind fellow-prisoner of Harry, named Max, also arranged with the guards for Lore to sleep on her father's usual palliasse, laid directly on the damp ground next to him. Her intermittent slumber, however, was frequently interrupted by the constant stream of men with agonising stomach cramps heading for the latrines. In the morning, half-awake and very hungry, she did not want to be roused and return to the nightmare world of the camp, the sick prisoners and her arguing parents.

It was not Blind Max who eventually made her wake up, but his brother – a young rabbi named Ansbacher – a prisoner who was also a refugee from Belgium. Instead of talking about God and divine will, he told her that she was the bravest girl he had ever met, and then added that Grete had died of pneumonia during the night. She was now at peace, he said, and Harry wanted to know whether Lore wished to see the body before she was buried that afternoon in the small cemetery outside the camp where the Spanish prisoners had been interred. What a question to ask a 12-year-old girl! Lore's answer was an emphatic negative because she wanted to remember her mother not as a lifeless corpse, but as the dynamic woman who never gave up, even when all the odds were against her. That afternoon, Ansbacher acted the part of father to Lore, standing beside her and offering words of comfort in the cemetery as the corpse, wrapped in a bedsheet, was lowered into the hastily-dug grave. Beside them, Blind Max had to support Harry, consumed by his own sense of loss and overwhelmed by guilt for causing Grete's death. At that moment, Lore hated him for not being a strong and caring parent for his distraught daughter. It was a long time before she could really forgive him.

Had there been a woman present, maybe Lore could have explained to her the confusion in her mind as she wandered around the little cemetery, staring at all the strange Spanish names on the gravestones. But there were just the three men and an armed guard waiting at the cemetery gate. Eventually, she approached her father,, who took her in his arms. She did not resist but was unable to weep with him while Ansbacher recited *Kaddish* – the Hebrew prayer for the dead – of which she understood not a word. She felt vaguely ashamed, as though failing to weep like her father was dishonouring Grete, who lay, wrapped in the bedsheet at the bottom of the grave. Rabbi Ansbacher talked to a representative of the Jewish community in Perpignan, present for the funeral, about the possibility of having Lore adopted by a family there who had volunteered to look after her. Harry roused himself to agree this would be best for his daughter, but Lore refused to be separated from her father in case he too died, leaving her completely alone in a country where she could not even speak to her adoptive family, however nice they might be. That sounds perfectly logical, but there was no conscious reasoning behind it, just panic.

The guards allowed this confused and unhappy 12-year-old girl to spend the night on a straw mattress laid next to Harry's on the damp sandy ground. Lore, having lost any sense of time, with her prized wristwatch now worn by a Nazi woman in Germany, spent hours shivering from the cold and damp. She wondered what Grete – whom she had only seen laugh or cry on a couple of occasions – had been like as a person. Having been raised at first by her faithful nanny Anna and later by Harry, she had only known her mother one-to-one when she was coping with the stresses of their life as refugees and increasingly ill herself. Had Grete ever laughed out loud and been happy like other girls' mothers? Lore wondered. What had been her likes and dislikes? Had she been pleased to give birth to a daughter, or disappointed that her only child was not a little boy? Now, she would never know the answers to a million questions she would have liked to ask the person who had been known as Dr Grete Schindler.

Chapter 7

The nightmare of Gurs

After a few days of Lore being the only female person in the camp at St Cyprien, all was chaos as 3,870 prisoners collected the few belongings they had been able to keep and were hustled by the guards into a long queue by the main gate. The drinking water at St Cyprien was now also polluted by sewage from the latrines, everyone had diarrhoea and 112 confirmed typhoid cases had to be transferred to a hospital in Perpignan. Heavy downpours having flooded the camp so severely that several people drowned, the entire unhappy community was to be moved to the far western end of the Pyrénées, where the largest French concentration camp was near a village called Gurs. Rounded up like cattle, the prisoners were loaded onto soft-topped lorries for the short journey to the railway station, where a long train of cattle trucks was waiting.

The camp at Gurs had been built in 1939 under the Radical Socialist government of Edouard Daladier to accommodate 27,350 Republican soldiers and their dependents and members of the International Brigades who fled across the Pyrenees to France at the end of the Spanish Civil War in what was known as *la retirada.* The frontier ran from peak to peak along the mountain chain and Gurs was a mere fifty miles north of it. The refugees were fleeing literally for their lives. South of the Pyrenees, General Franco's fascist soldiers were lining up thousands of men, women and children every day for mass executions.

Although France was prepared to accept this influx of men, women and children, the Ministry of the Interior made it clear from the outset that the Spanish refugees were not to be given asylum, but rather treated as 'military members of an interned army'. So they had to be locked up behind barbed wire and not be allowed to travel farther into France or to settle anywhere as civilians. The decision was particularly ironic since France prided itself on being a *pays d'accueil* since the Revolution proclaimed the First Republic in 1789-99, with a policy of welcoming political refugees from the monarchist states of Europe.

Driven to the nearest railway station, the nearly 4,000 desperately sick prisoners were summarily dumped and herded into the long line of cattle trucks. The doors slammed shut and locked from the outside, Lore panicked in the darkness, finding it hard to breathe, surrounded by sick men groaning like animals and weeping. Like them, she had to relieve herself on the floor of the truck. The darkness and stench seemed never-ending as the train rolled west for a few hours, then waited in a siding while more important traffic used the line. In this stop-start manner the day passed and the following night also. At last, daybreak on 30 October saw the doors opened at the station in Pau. Not for the prisoners was there any sight of the mountains as they were herded by the armed guards out of the trucks and into lorries taking them to the enormous camp of Gurs. It stretched for a mile and a half on both sides of a country road and was half a mile wide. The camp was surrounded by six-foot-high double-barbed-wire fences with armed French gendarmes patrolling between them. In several languages, notices warned the newcomers that the guards had orders to shoot to kill, should anyone try to escape.

Although the demarcation line separating the German-occupied zone of France – part of Hitler's Atlantikwall that stretched from Norway to the Spanish border to block any invasion – was only twenty miles or so to the west, there were normally no German soldiers or SS men in Gurs or near it. Not until 18 July 1942[1] did SS *Hauptsturmführer* Theodor Danneker, head of Dept IV (Jewish Affairs) of the *Sicherheitspolizei* in Paris, who worked with Eichmann and Heydrich, pay the first of four visits to Gurs. Since the Vichy administration also had its Commissariat Général aux Questions Juives (CGQJ), run by rabid anti-semite Xavier Vallat, Danneker was very happy with the degrading conditions in Gurs and left the camp administration to carry on, somewhat disappointed in that he had been expecting to find there 20,000 Jews to deport and murder as his contribution to the Final Solution.[2]

Within the perimeter, six-foot-high barbed wire also separated the thirteen blocks into which the camp was divided. Each block comprised twenty-five wooden barracks holding sixty prisoners. Four blocks, designated J, K, L and M, made up the women's part of the camp, where nearly 10,000 women and children were confined in barracks generally better looked after by the inmates than the men's accommodation, as the women were accustomed to cleaning their homes and using their dressmaking skills to mend clothes. The dressmakers among them even made new ones from surplus pillow slips and mattress covers they managed to 'find'. Most were Jewish foreigners who had been living in France for many years without securing French citizenship under the assumption that the French government would protect them from any German invasion, only to find that Marshal Pétain's government in Vichy was nearly as anti-semitic as Hitler's government in Berlin. After its Statut des Juifs, published in the press on 19 October 1940, Jews were banned from any official job, including teaching, and foreign-born Jews were immediately interned in concentration camps. Both in the occupied zone and the free zone, the personnel staffing the camps were French. Vichy's attitude was apparently motivated by Pétain's belief that collaboration all the way with Hitler would persuade him to liberate the 1.5 million French soldiers locked up in German PoW camps. It did not: they stayed there until the end of the war.

The camps in Vichy France were not initially called 'concentration camps', but *centres d'hébergement,* or accommodation centres. Some were even referred to as *centres d'accueil* – welcome centres. Few French civilians during the German occupation of the north and, eventually, the southern zone too had the energy to worry about the places of detention for foreign refugees, whatever they were like; it was hard enough to get by each day with all the rationing, shortages of food and fuel caused by the German requisitions, the restrictions

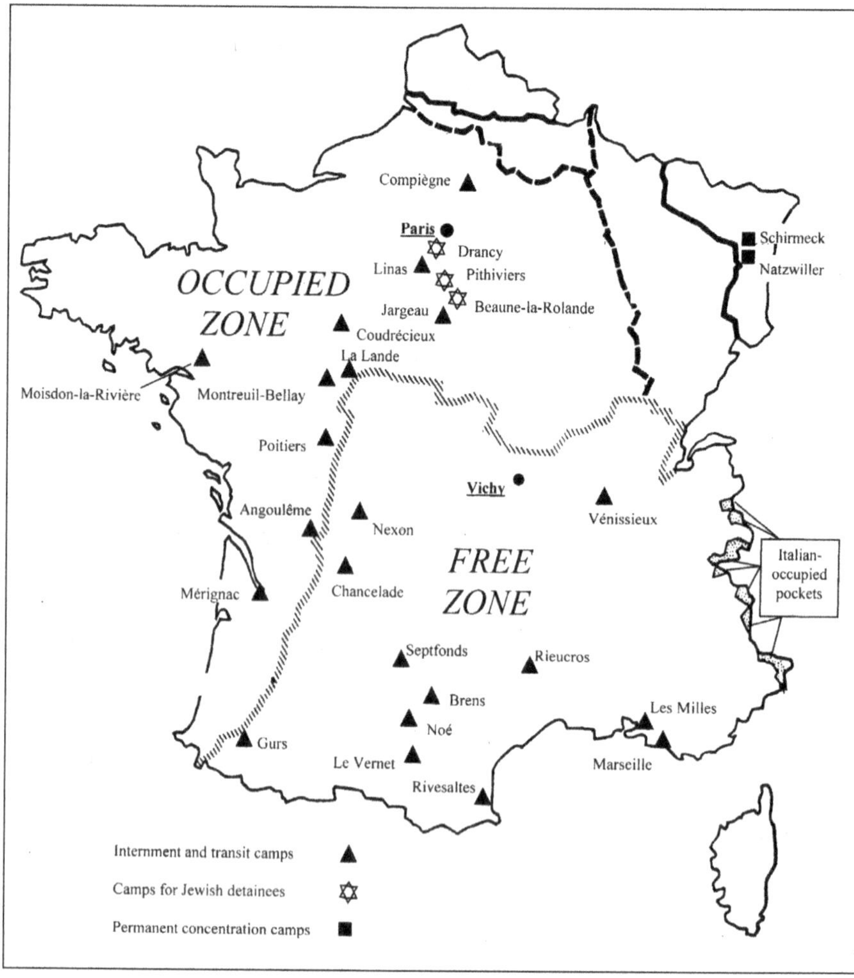

Location of German camps in the occupied zone and French camps in the so-called free zone by 1942

and the very real dangers of everyday life for ordinary citizens. It has been estimated that, despite the politically polarised fantasy of film depictions dividing the population equally into good *résistants* and bad collaborators, 98 per cent of the population – including especially those with children – took neither side, but just wanted to survive the next weeks and months.[3]

In each women's barrack at Gurs one prisoner was appointed the manageress – a job for which she had no desire and no training.

It was left to her to deal with the severely depressed and the occasionally hysterical fellow prisoners. Another unsought task was the preparation of lists – by age-groups of children, the aged and the pregnant, by nationalities and by religion – to satisfy the camp bureaucracy. Although the male blocks were guarded by gendarmes, the women's blocks were guarded by locally-recruited girls from peasant families, many of whom took pleasure in tormenting the educated townswomen in their charge.

Lore, as the only female among the new arrivals, was immediately separated from her father. In the women's blocks 9,771 adults and children of both sexes up to the age of 15 or 16 were confined. Any older male adolescents were then sent into the men's blocks. The remaining children all had mothers looking after them, but Lore was alone, with no one to care for her. Staring anguishedly after the disappearing figure of Harry, she was escorted by two armed gendarmes – they seemed to her menacingly tall – to one of the crowded women's barracks, where she was not welcome because there was no space for her. Terrified, hungry and thirsty, she collapsed, failing to understand where she was, or why. Although 12 years old, she was so thin and under-developed that everyone thought she was 10 or 11 at the very oldest. Presumably for this reason, and the lack of any parent to care for her, after a few days she was placed, not in the 200-bed hospital at the other end of the camp, but in a kind of infirmary adjacent to her barrack.

It was run by a prisoner who had been a hospital nurse before she was arrested. Schwester Käte ruled it with a rod of iron and only a modicum of medicines or even bandages. She did, however, persuade Lore to eat and drink until she had the strength to take advantage of the fact that the infirmary was not inside any block and therefore unguarded, leaving her free to wander along the central road of the camp, desperately searching for her father. Being so near the Atlantic and the mountains, Gurs had downpours of rain almost every day. Constructed on a subsoil of clay with no natural drainage, the whole camp was knee-deep in mud. As footwear, most prisoners wore ill-fitting home-made clogs fashioned from spare wood, crudely shaped for the soles, uppers fashioned from flattened tin cans and string to tie upper and sole together. These were continually being sucked off their feet by the mud. A few women who managed to procure rubber knee-boots from outside volunteered to fetch the rations and even carried the more elderly women piggy-back style to the latrines. One night, an elderly woman who needed to relieve herself in the middle of the night fell, was unable to raise herself, and drowned in the mud. One problem for the women solved itself. With the very inadequate diet most of them ceased to menstruate. At first worried – how could they possibly be pregnant? – they were reassured by doctor-prisoners that this was quite normal in conditions of near starvation in the camps in Germany and Poland.

In the men's part of the camp, some prisoners died from rare beatings by the guards, but most deaths there and in the women's blocks were from disease and prolonged malnutrition. Some prisoners who had been able to smuggle in money bought extra food from the many black marketeers who sprang up among other prisoners, the Spanish workers, the guards and local people. The newspaper *Indépendant des Basses-Pyrénées* reported on 5 November 1941 the sentencing of a guard who, after taking 1,000 francs from two prisoners to assist their escape, betrayed them and kept the money they had given him; on 27April 1942 another guard was sentenced after being found in possession of three ration cards; on 15 June 1942 a third guard was sentenced for selling food to prisoners at grossly inflated prices. The regional newspaper *Echo d'Oloron* reported on 30 January 1942:

> The camp at Gurs continues to be the haunt of gangsters exploiting the misery of the inhabitants. Recent arrests of those exploiting the needs of the prisoners by selling goods and services at exorbitant prices, include a caterer and his wife, a pork butcher offering to help would-be escapers and also selling ration cards, two guards who

> acted as go-betweens, a restaurant owner and three prisoners.

Prisoners with funds wanted mainly food, but also wood for heating. Clothes and medicines could sometimes, but not always, be obtained from the various charity workers inside the wire. The main concern of the black marketeers was to deal in small articles that could not easily be detected by the sentries at the gates. High on the list were chickens' eggs, slices of sausage, ham and bacon, and fat that could be spread on bread. Slices of alleged chicken were often taken from the cooked carcasses of dogs, cats and even foxes. Small tins of sardines and tuna were especially prized because they could be re-traded, as was anything sugary, like jam, dates and figs. In the demand-driven economy of the camp, the black-market prices of some items reached between three and ten times the legal prices in the civilian population. Many prisoners lacking money used anything of value they could find to buy food: rings and other jewellery, wristwatches and even fountain pens all had their negotiable values. Some women were reduced to selling themselves in order to improve their, or their children's diets, but this cannot have been easy because of the lack of privacy.[4]

In Gurs, a full stomach was no guarantee of survival: prisoners also died from epidemics that included dysentery and typhoid fever, although they were officially warned not to drink any water that had not been boiled. Typhus, too, claimed many victims, its vectors being the ubiquitous body lice. Finding one on her underwear one day, Lore was terrified. She tore the garment off and rubbed and rubbed it under a cold water tap in the outside washbasins, desperate to get rid of any trace of the insect. Adults and children died each day and the sight of corpses being transported, stacked on an open truck like oversize logs, to the cemetery outside the wire was a daily occurrence. Eventually a total of 1,067 prisoners would be buried there. Attendance at funerals represented one of the few possibilities of leaving one's block with a pass. Brief notes would be passed or thrown across one or more barbed-wire fences at the end of the blocks, asking a spouse, relative or friend in another block to attend the interment of a total stranger so that a meeting could take place, because the guards never checked everyone's relationship with the deceased.

Young as she was, Lore knew that, if the louse had bitten her, she could swiftly have become yet another body being carted off to the cemetery. Like everyone else's, her hair was infested with nits or head lice, but they were a different species, which irritated and did no permanent harm. Her worst hygiene problem was the scabies caused by tiny mites that burrow into the skin to lay their eggs. They made her whole body itch, especially at night. Nearly everybody at Gurs was infested with them. There was just one plague of fleas as well, in the summer of 1939. Where they came from, no one ever knew. In the daytime they hid in the cracks between the timbers of the huts. The alarmed camp administration used hundreds of gallons of bleach to treat every crack in each hut. Bodily examinations revealing bite marks resulted in individual prisoners having their clothing fumigated or burned, during which time the sufferer was kept in isolation, wrapped in a blanket. The single blanket issued to each prisoner was totally inadequate. The barracks, having been constructed for male Spanish prisoners to use in summer weather, with no insulation and many cracks where draughts entered, were impossible to heat. So most of the women slept with all their clothes on under their single blanket in the endeavour to be warm enough. This, of course, was bad for hygiene.

The separation of all men in other blocks – ostensibly to preserve 'decency' was particularly hard to bear when a child was ill. As Hannah Schramm commented in her history of the time she spent as superintendent of Block M in the camp at Gurs, it was particularly cruel for elderly women separated from their aged and maybe handicapped husbands in a different block.[5] In one barrack a delegation from the Secours Suisse found several old and skeletal men huddled around a stove in which they were burning the straw from the palliasses on which they had to sleep in a desperate effort to keep warm.[6] Occasionally, news from Gurs appeared in Jewish papers in Switzerland and the USA, inciting the commandant of the camp – who insisted everything was normal, with just the occasional suicide – to give instructions for more rigorous censorship of all outgoing mail. In August 1940 Hannah Schramm praised the volunteer nurses she met:

> Our four nurses were magnificent. 20-year- old Doris distributed what medicines she could and accompanied the doctors on their rounds. In fact, each day she had to run one-and-a half miles to the main hospital and collect half the necessary medicines, stop at each block's infirmary on the return journey, begging for whatever medicine they could spare, and repeat this in the afternoon. Paula, a chubby little woman, was extremely kind. Annie was the wife of an orchestral conductor and a singer. These two were perpetually on the go between the beds and the toilets, washing the patients, emptying the bedpans and cleaning soiled bedding. It was a labour of Sisyphus.[7] They also had to find water for the stoneware hot water bottles the sick kept in their beds, which had to be heated in Stone Age fashion, in a pit surrounded with hot stones, if the nurses could get the fire to draw by using their lungs as a bellows. Stephi, the fourth nurse, came from Austria. Her genius was the ability to make light and tasty meals from very little.[8]

For the ordinary prisoners, the day's rations consisted in the morning of a cup of acorn coffee and a slice of bread that had to be eaten before the rats got it. These animals were very persistent and even crawled under the blanket of a sleeping child or adult to steal bread tucked under the arm of the sleeper. They were not town or sewer rats, but *surmulots* or large black field rats native to the area of the camp before it was built, and which bred rapidly thanks to the scraps they found.

Emboldened by sheer numbers, they stole food left unattended for a moment despite the presence very close of the prisoners. If some of them lived in their normal habitat, in tunnels in the neighbouring fields and woodland, others made their homes underneath the barrack floors. After the ubiquitous mud, they were the worst scourge of Gurs, chewing holes in unguarded clothing to use the bitten-off cloth in making their nests. On a few occasions, they also attacked elderly and infirm prisoners in their sleep, inflicting numerous bite marks on their legs.[9]

At midday and in late afternoon, the 'meals' were often just mugs of tasteless soup in which floated a few slices of carrots, some chickpeas or lumps of swedes which, before the war, had been fed to cattle. A letter from a prisoner in Gurs, which somehow escaped the censors, was published, in the Swiss newspaper *Basler Nachrichten* of 12 February 1941, containing these lines: 'I await death by starvation, having lost 56 pounds in weight since my incarceration, tortured by the cold … I can hardly find the strength to stand up.' The other hunger most prisoners suffered was for news of the world outside the wire. Old catalogues were pored over, especially those with illustrations, and the rare newspaper that made it into the camp was passed from hand to hand among prisoners desperate to know what was happening in the world that might affect their chances of being released. There was a sports ground, to which the female prisoners theoretically had access, but it was mainly used by the men – less frequently as the poor diet deprived them of the necessary energy.

With their husbands so near and yet so inaccessible a few hundred metres distant in the men's blocks, married women worried about their menfolk's health. 'Who is looking after him now?' they wondered. As the bodies on the cart carrying the day's corpses to the cemetery testified, men died more frequently than women. The reason was unclear, as it still is. Were the men less accustomed to looking after themselves and keeping their barracks clean? Certainly, the women kept themselves more active than their spouses, who tended to become so demoralised after a few weeks that some of them did not even bother to collect their rations.

Lore finally found Harry with some of the men who had shared the terrifying journey in cattle trucks from the camp at St Cyprien. For whatever reason, he had regained some interest in the world and amused himself and the other prisoners by drawing cartoons of camp life on paper acquired through a guard. He seemed to Lore almost like his old self: the *Vati* she had loved before he was taken off to Sachsenhausen. His caricatures of fellow prisoners even made her laugh sometimes. On another day he would change and sink back into his blind depression, asking Lore the same question again and again: 'Do you blame me for causing your mother's death?'

Anguished by his repeated question, she refused to answer and ran back to the infirmary.

Chapter 8

Of lipstick, hairdos and passes

Sleeping on a camp bed in the infirmary and with Schwester Käte ensuring that she ate her meagre rations, Lore stopped losing weight, but was still painfully thin. She also lost some of the mindless panic and terror that had afflicted her since coming to Gurs. When a prisoner-doctor judged her fit enough, by the standards of the camp, to leave the infirmary, Schwester Käte found Lore a job, to justify keeping this thin and desperate girl under her personal care. It involved carrying the filled bedpans of the sick patients through the mud to the latrines and there climbing up the soiled steps – many sick women did not make it to the top in time – to empty them. The latrines were a line of cubicles with no doors and no toilet paper, each with a hole in the floor and nowhere to sit, which meant crouching down and hanging onto whatever support was within reach. They were raised up on a platform to accommodate a line of dustbins placed one below each hole. Every day a donkey cart was driven up with a couple of Spaniards on board, who lifted the filled dustbins onto it and replaced them with empty ones. Then it departed for the full ones to be emptied into ditches outside the camp. Some women who could not manage to relieve themselves whilst in full view of the world would ask a friend to stand in front of them as a living screen while they were up there. Or, as Hanna Schramm, who arrived at Gurs aged 46, put it like this in her memoir of living at Gurs:

> It was easy to miss the hole, so some prisoners including me volunteered to clean the floor each day with a crude brush of stiff grass dipped in a solution of creosote. We eventually got used to all this, but it remained disagreeable

> psychologically and physically difficult. In contrast with the primitive latrines, many of the women sought out a fellow-prisoner who had been a hairdresser in civilian life. The woman sleeping on the next *paillasse* to me was one, and never lacked for customers. Prisoners who had been manicurists, masseuses and dressmakers were all kept busy in this unlikely environment. Some women slept on their *paillasses* with their hair in borrowed curlers. A lucky few, who had been able to keep or buy some lipstick or nail varnish did their best to keep up appearances.[1]

In the men's blocks, the only prisoners able to earn money regularly, with which to buy food, were former watch-menders, cobblers and tailors, whose services were always in demand. Women prisoners handy with a needle and scissors grabbed any material they could and made clothes for their fellow sufferers and also to sell to the peasants outside.

Eventually lack of space in the infirmary obliged Schwester Käte to tell Lore to go back to her barrack. There, with all the mothers understandably taking care of their own children and even stealing food for them, she might have starved literally to death had not two adult sisters adopted her. Elsie and Marthe Liefmann came from Freiburg in south-west Germany, just twenty miles from the pre-war border with French Alsace. Robert Wagner, the fanatical Nazi Gauleiter of Baden-Württemberg, had taken advantage of France's defeat to annex the neighbouring French province of Alsace into his *Gau*, renamed Gau Westmark. Working together with his equally fanatical deputy Josef Bürckel, he expelled all the Jews in the expanded *Gau* by dumping them on France in what he dubbed *die Wagner-Bürckel-Aktion*, to make it sound like a military operation. The date was deliberately chosen to be at the end of Succot. Between 22 and 24 October 1940, some 6,638 of these unfortunates ended in Gurs, making Wagner and Bürckel Nazi heroes who had achieved for Gau Westmark the coveted title of *judenrein*, meaning 'cleansed of Jews'.

All the women were transported in cattle trucks to Oloron station and thence in lorries to Gurs. They arrived in the night and were helped down to the ground by guards according to the spare places in each block. Those who were aged or ill had to be helped to walk under a ceaseless downpour. The kitchen women had re-lit the fire beneath one of the cauldrons to ensure at least a cup of hot tea for the new arrivals, but there was no food. The newcomers who had no idea where they were and feared that the camp was run by the Gestapo, were reassured by the residents that they were in France with no German guards. They were not otherwise welcomed by prisoners who were supposed to move to another block and refused to leave the miserable piece of floor that had become their home to make room for anyone else. Accommodating the new arrivals had to be done by the prisoners, or more exactly by the prisoner-manageresses of the barracks and blocks.

One small and bossy woman who buzzed with energy announced that all the new arrivals – whether old and fearful or younger women accompanied by their children and young mothers with babies – had to record their names and former addresses, dates and places of birth before anything else.

In the service barrack, pencil in hand, she asked a fearful old lady, 'Where are you from?'

'Mannheim.

'And your last address in France?'

'I've never been in France. Is there a hotel here? Are you from the police?'

'No. You are at the internment camp at Gurs in the Basses Pyrénées.'

'Does the Gestapo come here?'

'It's a French-run camp and nothing is going to happen to you. Date and place of birth?'

'I was born on 11 May.'

'Of what year?'

The old lady had to think a moment, then, 'In 1868 at Heidelberg.'

'Last address?'

'The old people's home in Gailingen.'

'How did you get here?'

'Three days ago, the police came very early in the morning and gave us one hour to pack our bags and be ready to leave.'[2]

In some towns of Gau Westmark with more humane mayors, food shops were ordered to serve the departing Jews before other customers so that they might at least have food for two days on their journey. Others had to take whatever was already in their homes, however inadequate that was. As to their destination, they had no idea where they were being sent until the deportation trains stopped at the French border. There they were obliged to change their marks for French francs at a quite reasonable rate and were warned by the SS guards on the trains that anyone concealing an excess above the 100-mark limit per person would be shot when they were all body-searched. Thousands of German notes were burned on the spot, only a few courageous, or foolhardy, people daring to hope they could conceal some extra money. In the event, in order to adhere to its schedule, the train departed before anyone could be searched They had been allowed to bring only what they could carry, everything else having to be signed over to the Nazi state and the keys to their dwellings handed to the arresting officer.

With the rest of the convoy arriving and dumping its passengers, men and women in the different blocks, in the darkness and rain, priority was given to bringing them under cover and rescuing their suitcases and bundles of belongings from the mud. Some of the prisoners bestirred themselves to help the newcomers find the barrack to which they had been allotted; others watched emotionlessly as the soaked, confused and fearful crowd of women and children allowed themselves to be shown to places where they could spend the rest of the night, politely thanking anyone who helped them and nervously trying to keep an eye on their belongings. Among the crowd were sick and injured people on stretchers and even a few who were insane and had been arrested in mental hospitals. One old lady of 95 was screaming for her suitcase and refused to be helped under cover before it was retrieved and brought to her because her family photographs were inside, including a picture of her son who was in Dachau concentration camp – whether dead or alive, she did not know. As the night wore on, more and more women and children arrived, and lorries transporting their husbands and older sons passed en route to the men's blocks.

The camp was often a whirl of disturbed people, confused by rumours and contradictory regulations, but never more so than the night when Hanna Shramm said goodnight to the other prisoners who had taken the initiative of helping the new arrivals from Gau Westmark. She returned to her barrack, climbing over suitcases, shoes and discarded clothing on the floor to find her precious personal space encroached upon from all directions. The next morning was a different chaos. Some suitcases lay still in the mud unclaimed, their contents soaked. If the owners found them, they rejoiced. But some, perhaps the property of prisoners too sick or bewildered to claim what was theirs, were left for two or three days by the central roadway of the camp and then opened by profiteers, who sold off the clothing and anything else of value at inflated prices.

Hanna Schramm noted how Gauleiter Wagner's victims, who were mainly from tradesmen's families, busied themselves to create a sort of home space in the barracks, creating tasty-smelling soup from scraps of food they had brought along, many of them having to be warned not to try cooking inside the barracks for risk of fire. But some seemed to have lost the will to live. One young teenager in Hanna's barrack sat all day without moving or speaking, gazing into space. Of poor health, she had been looked after by an older sister, who had been absent when the arrests were carried out, leaving her unable to relate to other people. She was eventually taken to the outside washing facilities and washed by kindly neighbours, her hair combed and clothing tidied. Her only reaction was to weep copiously.

A few weeks later she was transferred to an asylum, diagnosed as having incurable melancholia, i.e., depression.

Another woman, who had lost her mind after losing her baggage, ran from barrack to barrack, accusing other prisoners at random of having stolen it and grabbing anything she thought she recognised until it was torn from her hands by the owner, which was not easy as she fought tooth and nail to keep what she thought was her property. Increasingly distraught, foaming at the lips, she was eventually subdued by six other women who forced her to go to the infirmary where a doctor wanted to inject a sedative but could not keep her still long enough. She was eventually tied into a straitjacket, where, spitting hatred in all directions, she more resembled a caged animal than a person. Although there had been no other choice, Hanna felt ashamed of her part in subduing this poor creature. Another woman was taken away to an asylum for several weeks before returning cured, somehow accepting her fate of imprisonment for no crime. Yet others remained irritable, forever picking fights and disturbing the whole barrack. Some eventually calmed down; others remained unpleasant, leaving Hanna to conclude that they always had been like that in civilian life.

Most of the younger children who had arrived with their mothers seemed to take it all in their stride. Completely out of control, they ran about outside and inside the barracks when it rained, gradually losing much of their natural energy with the poor food. And what about the elderly? Of the 1,400 women in Hanna's block, at least 400 were over 60 and the oldest was 95. Some were blind, or nearly so. Others were totally deaf. Almost all had health problems that needed attention and medicine that was not available. Since they had to go outside to wash themselves with cold water in the wind and rain, there was no way of getting warm again. And the trek through the mud at night to reach the latrines was fatal for more than a few; several of the elderly broke bones when falling in the dark. A solution to that was invented by placing an empty catering-size food can at the end of each barrack, where they could relieve themselves without going outside. A common fear among the elderly was of dying in the camp and being consigned to the bleak cemetery just outside the wire.

When someone did die, the body was laid out in the barrack and washed by two women. Why? wondered Hanna, watching them at work. It made no difference in the world of misery and mud that was Gurs. But custom demanded this last service to the departed, usually with a group of women watching and congratulating themselves that they too were not laying there naked, cold and stiff. The women preparing the body debated whether to remove the false teeth or leave them. The barrack supervisor wrote out a death certificate, countersigned by the nearest doctor, and the dead woman's pitiful belongings were collected for handing over to the camp commandant's office, in case they were claimed by a surviving relative. The small bundle contained the dead woman's wedding ring, some underwear, carefully stitched where it had given way after long wear, and a worn dress. From a pocket in the dress, Hanna took an envelope postmarked New York. It began, *Liebe Mutti.* Dear Mother! She put it in her pocket, needing the address to write back to the unknown daughter in America. Another of the old women took out a prayer book and began intoning prayers for the dead.

The oldest and least able women were grouped together, by their fellow-prisoners, in barracks where repeated representations to the camp administration obtained some camp beds for them – a luxury compared to the palliasses stuffed with rotten grass or straw laid on the barrack floor, on which the others had to sleep. Incredibly, since all the prisoners were in the same boat, the newcomers known as *Badoises* suspected that the women already imprisoned were criminals, asking themselves why otherwise would they be living like animals in these damp and leaky barracks? Unbelievably, considering what we now know about the death camps in the east *and* the fact they had been arrested by German police and Gestapo men and women, the Badoises were constantly criticising the poor quality of the French administration of the camp. 'Back home in Germany,' they said, 'everything is so much better organised.' Indeed, it was, thanks to Himmler and his Allgemeine-SS corps of uniformed male and female murderers.

Organisation requires bureaucracy. When two women who had filled in all the right forms before the arrival of the newcomers were released to go to the still neutral USA, Hanna suddenly found herself in charge of 1,400 women in her block, for whom no preparation had been possible, since no one knew they were going to arrive until a few hours before they flooded in. Her office was a tiny room in the service barrack, which she shared with two assistants and the volunteer postmistress who, every weekday, no matter what the weather, ploughed through the mud in her rubber boots to collect the letters and parcels from the main gate. In the winter, each step required pulling the top of the rearward boot by hand to free it from the mud reaching almost to the top of the boot and then repeating the manoeuvre again and again and again. After half an hour of this, she was exhausted, soaked and covered in splashes of mud, and resigned herself to sitting for a couple of hours behind her little window distributing the mail to the fortunate few.

The only time in the whole day when these volunteers sat still was in the morning, when waiting for a male member of staff always addressed as 'Capitaine Montané', to whom they had to account for the 'business' of the block. He always arrived at the administrative barrack in the north of the camp fifteen minutes late with a squeal of brakes, but expected them to be ready and waiting, together with Mademoiselle Frézet, a French local government officer who deputised for the commandant. With Montané came his clerk, carrying the all-important rubber stamps, without which no document was valid. Montané was young, overweight and rude to the women, with a tendency to shout at the slightest lack of what he considered the respect due to him from them. The remedy was, for those courageous enough, to shout back at him. The four women often muddled papers for his signature, deliberately to confuse him about the number of passes he had signed, each permitting one woman to leave the block and search for a husband or a relative or a woman friend in another block. On one day, suddenly suspicious, Montané counted the signed passes and tore them all up, screaming that *nobody* might leave the block until further notice.

One of the women exploded, telling him that they were not jailbirds or criminals to be treated like this. Another joined in, saying he had no idea what it was like for a married woman to know her husband was, well or ill, just a short walk away, and adding that it was inhuman to deny her the chance of seeing him for a brief moment. If Montané's own mother were ill in another block, would he not need to go and see her? To their relief, he calmed down and apologised with ill grace, Mlle Frézet tapping him approvingly on the back, after which he announced that in future he would sign, not six passes a day, but ten. It was a small but important victory for the women.

Many prisoners accepted tasks in the administration of the camp, some from benevolence and others just to relieve the boredom. For some reason, it was hard to get anyone to peel and prepare the vegetables until someone had the bright idea of 'paying' the peelers and preparers of the vegetables with an extra ladle of soup each. There was a rush of volunteers.

Chapter 9

Mud, mosquitoes and music

Few prisoners had been given time when arrested to collect any winter clothing and suffered accordingly in the extremely harsh winter at Gurs when many refused to go outside, staying fully dressed day and all night in the overcrowded barracks, making perfect incubation conditions for viruses and bacteria and an ideal home for bugs and other vermin. The senior prisoner-doctor in the women's hospital ordered his staff to attempt to group together those already infected and isolate them, but this was often impossible if a woman had children or another person she was looking after, although herself ill. He wrote afterwards:

> Paralysed by the total absence of hygiene, we doctors had to grit our teeth and watch the progress of an illness travel from person to person. The absence of any building that could serve as a quarantine facility and the incredibly unhygienic conditions throughout the camp in the barracks and the latrines, the lack of disinfectants and medicines and the impossibility of providing a diet suitable for the sick – he reported to the camp administration in May 1941 *the daily ration amounted to no more than 500 calories per patient per day* – cancelled out all the efforts of the doctors and their helpers.[1]

If Gurs was a cold hell in winter, where nobody could get warm, with spring thousands of flies and mosquitoes emerged to torment the prisoners and guards alike. Some women had brought along a bathing costume – wherever did they think they were going? – and defied the flying insects in the endeavour to keep cool. Others stripped down to bra and pants until bullied to clothe themselves more 'decently' by the locally-recruited, strictly brought-up Catholic girls in charge of them, who dared not even wear sleeveless dresses, fearing accusations of immodesty. As soon as their backs were turned, the women prisoners stripped off their outerwear again.

Elsewhere in the camp, there were still nearly 6,000 anti-Franco Basques plus 9,000 Catalans and Republicans from other parts of Spain and a small contingent of communists and others from other countries, including the UK, who had volunteered to fight in the International Brigades during the Spanish Civil War.[2] With the recent influx of German-speakers and many Mosellanes, Austrians, Czechoslovaks, Poles, Yugoslavs, Romanians and Bulgarians, it was a Babel. The Basques and Spaniards acted as odd-job men in the women's blocks, repairing the leaks in the tarpaper roofs, which otherwise required a profusion of cans and pans and jugs to catch the drips each time it rained, which was nearly every day. As a favour, they would also hammer in a re-used nail or a rusty point snapped off from the barbed wire, on which to hang a garment out of reach of the rodents. The barbed-wire fences also served as clotheslines – there was nowhere else to hang a wet garment – with the result that clothing was often torn by the wind whipping it against the barbs and a friendly woman with a needle and some thread recovered from an old garment was asked to stitch the tear up.

Occasionally, one of the Basques would turn up with a piece of wood scrounged from another, unoccupied barrack and somehow fix it to the wall, making a theoretically safe shelf, on which to keep some food out of reach of the rats. Some of these men adopted a young single woman, bringing tidbits of food and sitting, holding hands with her, each of them whispering endearments that could not be understood by the other. When the girl's admirer was moved – one never knew why – to another block or another camp, she would often find another Spanish admirer. Incredibly, considering how little privacy there was, sometimes a baby resulted from these illicit liaisons, perhaps conceived in the long grass by the water tower. That was the only place in the women's sector of the camp where a couple lying down could find privacy, with the risk of disturbing rats, the entrance to whose burrow was concealed by the grass. The camp archives reveal a total of fourteen births in 1941 alone. Surprisingly, the camp administration provided an unused barrack, partitioned to provide pleasantly decorated individual bedrooms with proper windows and with flowers planted along the front of the building as a maternity block for mothers-to-be and some prisoners with very small babies.[3]

Elsie, the younger of the two sisters looking after their adopted niece, had been a doctor and reminded Lore in some ways of her own mother. Marthe was less practical, but more emotional and sympathetic. The two women took it in turn to stand in line to ensure that Lore received her rations and was able to consume them before anyone could steal them from her, and they also protected her from that invisible killer in the camps, solitude. Not to be alone in the world was literally a lifesaver for this anguished sub-teenager. With Elsie and Marthe, Lore learned again to laugh, to take pleasure in the beauty of a sunset and the sight of the snowcapped peaks to the south of Gurs, over which towered the majestic pic d'Anie, its snows turned pink by the setting sun. They taught her not to dwell on the twin fences of barbed wire and the armed guards patrolling between them, but to look beyond them and appreciate the beauty of nature all around.

Another miracle happened with the arrival of a small team from the Swiss Red Cross under a beautiful, Swiss-German trained nurse named Elsbeth Kasser, who became known as 'the angel of Gurs'. She had been working among French refugees in several camps near Toulouse when she heard of the conditions in Gurs and had what she called 'an intuition' that she was needed far more there. Julius C. Turner, a German artist prisoner, sketched her sitting in the sun in the peace of the cemetery when she was recovering from some illness. Tired and convalescent as she was at the time, her strength of character is apparent in the sketch. More dangerous for Turner were his depictions of the despairing groups of prisoners assembled for transport to 'unknown destinations', which had to be hidden from the guards. And Elsbeth was warned openly that she must show more consideration for the administration of the camp and not favour the detainees!

The Swiss organisation *Secours aux Enfants* (SOE) brought in supplies of powdered milk and canned food to supplement the diet of children, the elderly, young mothers and pregnant women. Each morning, Elsbeth invited children, including Lore, to drink milk and eat some Swiss cheese in the 'Swiss barrack' by the central road of the camp where she also kept a library of several thousand books in German for the prisoners to borrow and read. Lore took books back to her barrack, immersing herself in romances of young girls at their first ball or falling in love with a boy, to distract herself for a while from the horrors of the camp and the increasingly bitter winter weather of 1940-41. It was not easy to read in the barrack, with only three low-wattage bulbs for the whole building, and there were no windows to let daylight in, while opening the ventilation shutters at the top of the roof to let some light in also let in cold air. There was a perpetual battle between those of the sixty prisoners in the hut who wanted light, like her, and women who wanted warmth for themselves or their children, especially the sick ones. The single woodburning stove in each hut was grossly inadequate. The only fuel for it was wood, for which they had to forage outside the wire, leaving their children inside the camp as hostages,

Elsbeth's simple motto was: 'Instead of complaining about the darkness, let's switch on a light.' Before coming to Gurs, she had already worked for the Service Civil International in Spain during the Spanish civil war and volunteered for the *Cartel Suisse de Secours aux Enfants Victimes de la Guerre* during the Winter War in Finland after the USSR invaded this neighbouring country in 1939-40. For four months in bitter sub-zero weather, the tiny Finnish army held back the massive Red Army in a struggle that completely exhausted the defenders whose children certainly merited all the help they could get. At first the prisoners at Gurs suspected Elsbeth must be some kind of spy for the Pétainist régime. They were eventually won over by her obvious care for them and willingness to share their living conditions after she convinced the camp commandant to let her spend her nights inside the wire, having persuaded him that she would not cause problems but might resolve some for him.[4] Some help was also brought into the camp by the Dutch Red Cross and *Le Secours Protestant*, which was banned on 12 October 1942 as being 'too favourable towards the prisoners'. The American Joint Distribution Committee also worked in Gurs and other camps until the Axis powers declared war on the USA four days after the Japanese attack on Pearl Harbor. Even the parish priest of Gurs village managed to find and bring in some canned goods from time to time. The Quakers, as so often in times of crisis, collaborated happily with the other benevolent organisations, signalling their arrival in Gurs while Lore was there in December 1940 with a pre-Christmas delivery of 800,000 rations of food and medicines, especially favouring Block G, known as the Death Block.[5] After Christmas, other Quakers from Toulouse arrived with 2,000 rations for distribution to children, pregnant and breast-feeding women and others visibly losing weight. They also managed to spirit away, on the day before he was to be shipped off en route to Auschwitz, a Lithuanian doctor in the main hospital named Bachrach who had served with the International Brigades in Spain.

The Unitarian Service Committee also answered the call of conscience. There were two dentists among the male prisoners, who agreed to use a dental drill and some accessories provided by the Committee. It was of the type, common at the time, with an arrangement of belts and gears powered by pedalling to turn the drill head, but at speeds considerably slower than a modern dental drill and consequently producing more painful vibrations in the tooth being operated on. So many prisoners had dental problems that the two dentists took it in turns, one pedalling and the other operating, from morning to night. There was no local or general anaesthetic to fight the pain. More serious still was the lack of adequate sterilisation facilities, which meant that particles of one patient's caries were often transferred to another patient's mouth.[6] However, the main work of the charitable organisations present in the camp in the early months of 1941 was far more basic: purchasing vast quantities of bleach, with which to spray every crack between the woodwork to kill the vermin hiding there. But these were also concealed in people's clothes and inside their suitcases. So infested were virtually all the prisoners that any transferred to other camps were immediately isolated and disinfested, if possible. A description of the camp by a doctor prisoner during the winter when Lore was held there reads:

> The barracks were cold, wet and filthy. The prisoners slept on half-filled sacks of mouldy straw inhabited by lice, fleas and rats. [On arrival at the camp] our scant belongings were hurled off the lorries into the ubiquitous mud caused by the incessant rain. The ditches were full and overflowing.[7]
>
> If the camp population was reasonably healthy in summer, once winter took hold, diseases were rife. Due to malnutrition and the appalling hygiene generally, even that old killer tuberculosis reared its head, as did meningitis, almost always fatal in the children. But the commonest malady was variously labelled dysentery, gastro-enteritis or paratyphoid. Under whatever name, its combination of high fever and the loss of control of bladder and bowels could lead swiftly to death.[8]

Elsbeth Kasser's account included a description of the difficulty in establishing priorities in this hell where the guards did nothing to help and the running of the camp was left to former doctors and nurses among the prisoners and the volunteer prisoners who ran the canteens and laundries.

Amazingly, there was a vestige of culture in the camp. The prisoners included some professional musicians and singers, who gave recitals. There were also readings by poets reciting their own work, plays performed by professional actors and actresses and language and art lessons given by former teachers. In clement weather, children were seated on the grass between the barracks and given lessons approximating to normal schoolwork by imprisoned teachers. Prisoners also arranged language lessons. Among them were also lawyers and journalists. World-famous singers gave recitals; the last song was always 'Plaisir d'Amour' with its refrain 'Plaisir d'amour ne dure qu'un instant / Chagrin d'amour dure toute la vie'. The pleasure of love lasts but an instant / the sadness of unrequited love lasts all one's life. Instrumental musicians, including the leader of the Vienna Philharmonic, gave recitals on Sunday mornings. The YMCA procured stringed and woodwind instruments from somewhere for a prisoners' orchestra, as well as sheet music. There were also piano recitals, a string quartet, sonatas for violin and piano by Beethoven and other composers. Actresses without scripts improvised performances. Professional artists arranged exhibitions of their paintings.

One of them, named Edith Auerbach, somehow managed to obtain a donkey and a small cart, with which she toured the locality buying whatever vegetables the peasants would sell her and flirting with the guards on the main gate to distract them from examining what she was bringing in. When the daily ration amounted to 500 or 600 calories, prisoners ate anything from artichokes to swedes to cabbage and pumpkin. Naturally, there were rumours that the guards were stealing provisions meant for the prisoners, but there was strict rationing throughout France and many shortages were suffered by town-dwellers unable to cycle into the countryside at weekends and haggle with the peasants for anything they could spare. Inside the camp, it was a treat to have occasionally some rice or chickpeas, and a couple of potatoes was considered a luxury. The meat ration was officially 5 or 6 grams per person per day – a mouthful, if one could find it in the soup. Sometimes, the meat delivered to the prisoner-cooks was rotten; once a 40-kilogram delivery of stinking cow intestines had all to be thrown away; on another occasion 200 kilos of spinach was fermenting and inedible yet counted as consumable by the administration. Even the *préfet* of the Basses Pyrénées was moved to protest in June 1941 when he discovered that the daily ration inside Gurs was costed at less than 5 francs, notwithstanding an official allotment of 11.50 francs per person per day. Where did the difference go?

On some days a sort of impromptu market took place outside the main gate, but to buy any meat there legally required handing over a ration card and these were all taken away and used by the camp administration to purchase the official rations. It was the male prisoners, physically larger than the women and who had been accustomed to eating larger meals, who first showed the signs of gross malnutrition in the form of oedemas in the legs, arms, hands and even on the face. Their general debilitation saw them lying for longer and longer on their palliasses, without the energy to stand. In any case, their feet were too swollen to put on their shoes. Those who could still move about tried searching for edible food in the women's garbage. The hunger for news of the outside world when it arrived, with a former journalist reading the headlines in each barrack for a small fee, was rarely satisfied, because at that stage of the war German advances appeared unstoppable, seemingly sentencing the listeners to confinement until they died.

While some women bringing otherwise unavailable food into the camp did so benevolently, others developed a black market, charging several times as much as they had paid. The regional commander reported to the *préfet* of the *départment*, 'It is not rare to see an egg bought for 1.25 francs re-sold in the camp for 7 francs.'[9] Sheer desperation to overcome the horrors of life in Gurs produced in the more artistic prisoners a flowering of creativity, using a smuggled knife or even a sharpened nail to carve and fashion model aircraft, figurines in wood, chessmen, dice, rings and other 'jewellery', even bracelets laboriously created from strips of flattened tin cans. A few of the most inventive prisoners even tackled ceramics, modelling clay that had been dug out from under the mud, and fired in specially constructed, single-use kilns that fell to pieces on cooling.

Elsbeth had little time to appreciate all this. She focused first on the children, then the young adults, making sure they could sit down to at least one proper meal each day. She set up workshops for them and obtained gardening tools to start them growing their own food. She even managed to obtain some ducks and two sheep for the prisoners' 'farm', where they grew potatoes and other vegetables on the waste ground behind the barracks. Her greatest difficulty was remaining a silent witness to the round-ups preceding the despatch of convoys headed for 'unknown destinations', which meant the death camps in eastern Europe. At those times, she acted as a trusted family friend, taking rings, watches and other precious mementoes from a departing prisoner and giving them to his or her spouse in another block who was staying behind. Any more active role would have seen her immediately expelled from the camp. Indeed, some women working for the Secours Protestant, the social services and other organisations were banned from the camp for bringing in money or uncensored letters for the prisoners.

Although Elsbeth was aware of Lore, she made it her policy to have no favourites. There were, however, paradoxically with Vichy's formal approval, a few Jewish social workers at Gurs. If the idea of a social worker in a concentration camp sounds bizarre, these were no ordinary women. In 1940 Andrée Salomon of the *Oeuvre de Secours aux Enfants* – an organisation to help children under threat – sent Romanian-born Elisabeth Hirsch to Gurs. She was no stranger to concentration camps, having played a role in the amazing rescue of prisoners from a camp eight kilometres from the centre of Lyon in eastern France. The town of Vénissieux was the site of a concentration camp in a complex of factory buildings surrounded by five-metre-high walls. It was guarded by armed Vietnamese troops under French officers. Inside the walls, conditions were so hellish that, on one night alone, twenty-six detainees committed suicide. The official staff departed, leaving to volunteer workers of the ecumenical charity *Amitié Chrétienne* the dreadful job of drawing up lists of prisoners for deportation! It was soul-destroying work, because they could not save everybody.

They had to deal with 1,300 cases and decided to find foster homes for children whose parents had been, or were going to be, deported and murdered. They ignored their orders to ship all the detainees to Drancy for onward routing to Auschwitz and managed to save some 500 adults and 100 children by forging identity papers, altering them to show false ages, arranging escapes and sending 140 people to hospital with faked medical certificates. Many of the children were smuggled out of the camp, hidden in the beaten-up old Citroën car belonging to the Jesuit Abbé Alexandre Glasberg. An unlikely-looking hero, with his short, stout build and thick-lensed spectacles, Glasberg was himself a converted Ukrainian Jew who understood anti-Semitism all too well. Working with him in the camp was the Jesuit Father Pierre Chaillet, from whom Cardinal Archbishop Gerlier of Lyon learned all the gruesome details of conditions for the prisoners and approved the rescue action.

Even with his backing, nothing could be done to save the rump of 545 prisoners who were transported to Drancy but, on the night of 29 August 1942, the volunteers packed the camp bus with children and managed to get 108 of them to the Lyon headquarters of the Jewish Scout movement. There, twenty or so were kitted out with uniforms to look like any other scouts and guides being sent on a camping trip in remote countryside. Others were hidden in private homes, for the most part Catholic. Prefect Alexandre Angeli of Lyon furiously demanded that eighty-four named children be handed over. As the patron of Amitié Chrétienne, Cardinal Gerlier backed up the volunteers' refusal to divulge names, after first prudently making a statement that he was nevertheless a loyal French citizen. To save his life, Father Chaillet was confined in a psychiatric clinic for three months, in conditions that were no better than they had been in the camp – Vichy had an appalling record for neglect and maltreatment of the mentally handicapped.

The camp at Drancy was infamous for shipping mothers off to extermination camps, anguished by the thought of their infants and small children being left behind in the care of four- and five-year-old siblings – all the children suffering often fatal diarrhoea from the food, which consisted mainly of cabbage soup. Drancy also had several sub-camps. One, in the heart of Paris and known as *Lager Ost*, was in what had been the very large Levitan furniture store. Requisitioned by the Germans, its first three floors were used as a vast sorting area for stolen Jewish property from pianos to teaspoons, to be sent to Germany. The fourth floor was a rudimentary dormitory for 795 poorly fed male and female prisoners from the main camp, who spent their days carefully wrapping and packing furniture, china, glass and more precious goods, often recognising among the loot their own personal treasures.[10]

Chapter 10

Goodbye to Harry

Neither of Lore's adoptive aunties, nor Lore herself, was aware that help for her was on the way. Born in Romania, at the age of 29 Elisabeth Hirsch had been naturalised French just before the outbreak of war, having worked in France since 1934 as a social worker, at first under Baroness Germaine de Rothschild, where her work included helping poor families to obtain basic necessities and medicines. After the French defeat, to this legitimate work was added the dangerous forging of identity documents and finding safe hiding places for Jewish children. With Elisabeth came two other OSE social workers to work inside the camp at Gurs.

Little-known in the English-speaking world, the Oeuvre de Secours aux Enfants, or Society to help Children, began in St Peterburg in 1912 as an organisation providing help, including medicine, for poor Jewish families who could not afford to pay doctors' fees in tsarist Russia. In the chaos of the civil war after the October Revolution, nothing in the vast area that had been Imperial Russia functioned normally, forcing the organisation to move its headquarters to Berlin in 1923 with Albert Einstein as its president, using the title OSE World Union. With the coming to power of the Nazis in 1933, OSE moved its headquarters for obvious reasons to Paris. After the French surrender in 1940 many of its personnel moved into the Free Zone, leaving enough colleagues behind to care for the 1,349 children in its several children's homes in the Occupied Zone.

Both refugees and resident Jews were subject to frequent round-ups that ended in Auschwitz and other death camps. The most infamous mass arrest took place in Paris on 16 and 17 July 1942 when, on orders from the Vichy government, 9,000 French police and gendarmerie officers arrested more than 13,000 Jews of all ages and confined most of them in the cycling stadium called Vélodrome d'Hiver, or Vel d'Hiv. The Germans had only asked for the arrest of those over 16 years of age, yet included among those arrested were some 4,000 children. The totally inadequate sanitation, lack of food and scarcity of even water led to suicides and one woman dying in childbirth while lying on the concrete floor during the five days before they were moved to transit camps en route to Auschwitz. Eugène Minkowski, the senior member of OSE in Paris, immediately gave orders to evacuate as many of the children remaining in OSE homes as posssible. As a result, about 5,000 of them were moved with the help of the Resistance into the Free Zone without the Vichy government being aware.

Everyone involved in this work was literally risking his or her life. The two other OSE women sent to Gurs with Elisabeth Hirsch were Ninon Haït-Weyl and Ruth Lambert, who explained the haphazard way in which the volunteers were recruited.

> On 24 October 1940 I was waiting on the platform of the station at Castelnaudary [about 50 kilometres to the east of Toulouse] and somebody pointed at a goods train, saying, 'There are Jews in those trucks.' I did not know what she was talking about.
>
> When the train for Lyon pulled in, I opened the door of my compartment at the same moment as the door of the next compartment was opened, and I found myself just inches away from Andrée Salomon. I had known her in 1931, just before her marriage. I had taken over her job, working as secretary in a lawyer's office. A brief exchange of words. She asked where I was going, adding, 'I really need you to help in the camp at Gurs.' Remembering the goods train at Castelnaudary, I realised what she meant. We swapped addresses. Arriving at Lyon in the blackout at 2 a.m., we went our separate ways.

> And in January 1941 Andrée was waiting for me at the station of Oloron Ste Marie. We stayed the night at the Hôtel Terminus. ('How come you're not dead?' they asked me when I went back there in 1946.) In the morning she introduced me to the management team. Seeing Ninon Haït, who had arrived a few weeks before me, I asked where I could take a shower. She replied, 'Stripped off, under the pump.' I didn't ask any more questions.
>
> I arrived at Gurs as a resident assistant working for OSE, and had half a barrack at the southern gate of the camp. The other half was lived in by the guards and their families. It took maybe three months before I got the other half of the barrack, and made a consulting room for the visiting doctors.[1]

Ruth devoted herself to alleviating the lot of the prisoners, somehow assembling a small collection of medical books and setting up a laundry. Occasionally she managed to take some of the children for an excursion outside the wire. She had to sail close to the wind in her dealings with the administration of the camp, but not overstep the limits. Of the black-uniformed guards, she said, 'They were swine, but we had to get along with them. I knew that Kaiser, the first director of the camp, had me watched all the time.'[2]

In 1942 Ruth was expelled from the camp for *acheminement clandestin de fonds et du courier au profit des hébergés* – forwarding money and uncensored letters to and from the prisoners. This was to avoid the strict censorship that opened every one of the 2,000 – 3,000 incoming and outgoing letters and parcels passing through the camp's postal system each day, in order to avoid the embarrassment to Pétain's government when prisoners' appalling descriptions of camp life appeared in Swiss and American newspapers. After January 1941 any money sent by post to a prisoner in Gurs was automatically confiscated by the administration.[3]

Ruth then went underground in the Resistance, continuing to work with the abbé Glasberg finding safe hiding places for Jewish children. After the end of the war, she worked under the umbrella of the United Nations Relief and Rehabilitation Administration (UNRAA) in displaced persons' camps inside Germany, many of them being former concentration camps. Following a lifetime of good works, she joined the convent of the Sisters of Prado in Lyon and there died on 17 November 1996, aged 82. Ninon Haït-Weyl had been a guide mistress in Alsace. She used the name Nicole Harcourt in the Resistance, where she belonged to the network known as *la Sixième.* She died at the age of 96 in Fontainebleau. Although born Jewish, converting to Christianity and becoming a priest, Glasberg continued during the Occupation to save Jewish lives, earning himself recognition at Yad Vashem as a righteous Gentile.

In the camp Elisabeth Hirsch used the name Henriette Ducom. The real Henriette was a social worker attached to the Mairie of Moissac in the Tarn-et-Garonne département. She had allowed her identity to be 'borrowed' and a copy of her ID card made with the photograph changed to the face of Elisabeth – an offence for which both women could have been immediately deported to a death camp, had it been discovered. The fake Henriette Ducom astonished Lore one day in January 1941 by coming to seek her out. This surprise visitor was dressed in a smart white linen suit, totally incongruous in all the filth and mud of the camp. She was young, attractive and, like all the OSE volunteers, very careful not to exceed her mandate. We don't know in which language she communicated with her young protégés in the Babel of Gurs who could not yet speak French and certainly not Romanian, Elisabeth's first language. Possibly, she had some knowledge of Yiddish, which was intelligible to German-speakers. Told, in whatever language, that Elisabeth was going to get her out of the camp, Lore did not at first believe this, because to do such a thing seemed impossible. Later, when Elisabeth had achieved the impossible, Lore called her 'my good fairy'.

The main problem for Lore was, of course, that leaving the camp would mean abandoning her father. Although Harry insisted that she must take any chance of escaping from Gurs, she could not bring herself to say goodbye to him. Vati, as she called him, was once more tender and loving. He could speak about Grete without breaking down and had stopped asking her that terrible question: was he responsible for her death?

Fate lent a hand at the beginning of February 1941. One morning Harry was in a group rounded up for transport to 'a better camp'. That was what the men had been told; in fact, the camp at Zoé, to which they were going, was an intermediate stop on the route to the assembly camp at Drancy near Paris, and from there to Auschwitz, but they did not know this. Harry really did seem to be thinking a little of the future and had even recovered his sense of humour, joking with Lore, '*Schlechter wie hier kann es doch nicht werden. Die Pension Noé muss doch eine Verbesserung sein.*' It can't really be worse than here, so the hotel at Noé must be an improvement.

On the morning of his departure, Lore waited anxiously at the main camp gate, hoping to at least catch sight of her father. While the open lorry with two guards armed with loaded rifles was halted for the sentries to check the identities of the departing prisoners, Harry found some inner reserve of courage to lean down and have that brief exchange with her – the last words they ever exchanged. As Lore remembered that farewell more than a half-century later,

> He also made me promise to come and see him at the camp at Noé and to write often, saying he would do the same. And he gave me one of his drawings, promising to send more from his new 'holiday camp'. Oh, Vati, I am so happy I found you again for that brief moment, even though it made the separation ahead of us infinitely harder! Over half a century later, I understand at last how it hurt so much to think about you that I tried, not really to forget you, but to replace you little by little with

Affix
stamp
here

Pen and Sword Books
c/o Casemate Publishers
1950 Lawrence Road
Havertown, PA 19083

living people who were not going to disappear from my life, and who represented a future for me. Please forgive me, you who were my real father and not a borrowed or adoptive one. You would have been so grateful to those extraordinary people who took your place and showed real love towards a daughter who was not theirs. You would have loved them as I have loved them all my life since then.

Oh, Vati, that was our fourth and final parting, for I never saw you again. Today, I think that perhaps you really were a strong man after all, for it must have taken such strength to call out that last encouragement to me despite the unbearable pain of leaving your child. You were not tough enough to stand the cruelty of the guards who tortured your body and your mind and you certainly lacked the burning courage of your wife, but you too were brave, you were good, you were gentle. No, I don't think you ever recovered the illusions about humanity and culture you had before being sent to the camp at Sachsenhausen, and later Rivesaltes, St Cyprien and Gurs – but I like to think that you found before dying a sort of calm that shielded you from the atrocious conditions of your last months.

Oh, Vati, were you ever able to believe again in your Heine, your Schiller, your Goethe and in your incomprehensible Schopenhauer? Not with the same naïve and unreasoning faith as before, but tempered with scepticism and reality, maybe. You see, after all I have lived through, I still believe today in the beauty of the world and in life, and I have that belief thanks mainly to those who took your place. I shall never know whether my hopes for you came true, but I should like to think so. When I parted from you that morning to go back to my hut and prepare for my own departure, what gave me

> the strength to think about my future just after saying goodbye to the only person I had in the world? I don't know, but perhaps through all the tears I wanted to be the girl you asked me to be with your, '*Haltung, Bummerl,'* for *Haltung* implies dignity and self-control.
>
> It is from that day that my terror of being separated from my loved ones dates, even when the separations are only temporary and for mundane reasons. From that day, to say goodbye – or, worse, to be separated from someone I love – has become for me a terror out of all proportion with reality. This is my worst wound from the war, which will never be healed. From that morning in February 1941 dates also my terror of losing those that I love. I don't mean just losing them to death, as is normal at my age now, but for the greater part of my life I have been afraid of disappointing and thus losing the people for whom I care. So, for the greater part of my life I have been tortured by the thought of causing the loss of those who have loved me as much as my parents did.[4]

As the lorry drove away to the railway station, Lore stared after it through her tears until it was out of sight. Coming to look for her and finding her crazed with despair, Elsie and Martha led her gently to the southern wire perimeter, to gaze at the beauty of the eternal, unchanging mountains until Lore gradually calmed down.

A couple of days later, early in the morning, Elisabeth assembled a group of children she was taking away from the camp but Lore could not go with them because she had no identity papers and therefore did not exist for the bureaucracy of Vichy France. At a loose end after her father's departure, did she attend the classes for children? We don't know. In fact, the attempts to teach the children anything in empty barracks were fairly useless because teachers arrived and left, the children had no textbooks or other reading material, and their mothers often made them do 'housework' instead of coming 'to school'.

The rations provided by the camp administration provided approximately two-thirds of the minimum calorific value necessary even for a child's normal health. In addition, some of the meat supplied was found on examination by the volunteer cooks to be out of date. One consignment was even infected by tuberculosis, despite certificates that it was sound from the abattoir at Navarrenx, whose veterinary inspector left his rubber stamp where anyone could use it. Also, the vegetables purchased locally were often loaded on carts by the peasants selling them in such a way as to conceal, under edible vegetables, others already rotten and inedible so that the inadequate diet was also lacking in vitamins.[5] So emaciated had Lore become that Elisabeth wanted to photograph her and publish the picture in order to provoke public sympathy for the camp inmates, but this was not allowed. Lore grew thinner and more fragile, exhausted by concentration camp life and increasingly troubled by her father's absence. Weeping for her mother too several months after Grete had died, Lore fell into despair at the thought of all the things that had happened to her in those few months. In addition to her malnutrition, which left her perpetually hungry, Lore's hair was increasingly infested with nits and her body covered with infected scabs where she had been bitten by bedbugs.

Lore finally left the camp after three months' delay, due to her lack of the right papers. So, from February to May, she was the only unaccompanied child among 15,000 prisoners in the immense camp of Gurs. Without Martha and her sister Elsie, life would have been impossible for this by now very unstable girl. During the delay, Lore was visited from time to time by Elisabeth, who called her 'the thinnest girl in the camp'.

At the beginning of May 1941 Elisabeth arrived at Lore's barrack one evening with the news that 'the thinnest girl' was leaving with her the following morning. How she arranged that, for a girl without official existence, Lore never knew. The answer is probably that a false ID card was forged for her. She was anyway torn by contradictory feelings. Leaving the camp meant regaining a more normal life where she would not be starving and could get rid of the lice and the scabies and sleep in a bed far from the huts, the barbed wire and the guards. She would be able to run where she wanted in the fresh air and not wade through the hateful mud or have to protect her bread ration from the rats. Perhaps, she thought, she would even go to school again with other children. That seemed like an impossible dream. Most of all, she wanted to visit her father, from whom she had received some obviously censored letters praising his 'new home'.

Elisabeth's news that she was actually leaving Gurs was a long-awaited miracle, but Lore was distraught at the idea of yet another goodbye when she left Martha and Elsie. With Grete dead and Harry gone, they had become her replacement relatives. They spent much of that last night holding her and gently but forcefully persuading her that going to live in a children's home outside the wire was a wonderful chance to go to school again, to be cured of the scabies and the lice and leave the hunger, filth, barbed wire, terror and mud of Gurs behind.

Early next morning, the children who were leaving had to go to the gate, where a truck was waiting to take them to Oloron St Marie, a little town near Gurs with a railway station. It seemed like a dream, but there indeed was the truck, with Elisabeth waiting beside it, smartly dressed as always. There were only four children leaving the camp: a boy called Erich aged 11 and two older children – Heinz, who was 14 or 15, and Ruth, the oldest. She was 17, and Lore learned later that her mother had lied about her age because only children under 16 could be saved by this rescue operation, restricted to younger children, which made Ruth very nervous. The other children were being seen off by their mothers and Lore was accompanied by Martha and Elsie, who had taken her parents' places. They had promised to write to her, but they never did. For fifty-five years she had no news of them until learning by chance that they had survived the war and were living in Switzerland.

Poor Ruth was terrified that a guard at the gate would discover the subterfuge, but all passed well and the camp disappeared into

Laure's mother Grete as medical student (above, right). Grete and Harry Schindler, on their wedding day (above, left). Grete and Harry when the reality of Hitler's racial laws already shows in her haggard appearance, but Harry still believes the Nazis cannot last. (below).

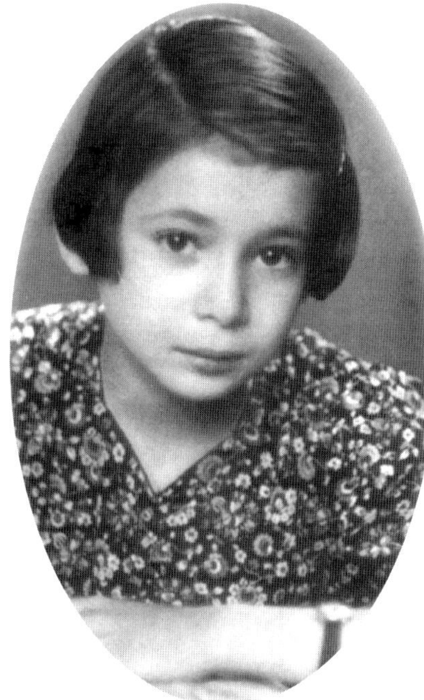

Laure aged four on a German Baltic beach in the summer of 1931 with her favourite doll (above, left). Aged nine, sporting her prized wristwatch in 1937 (above, right). Her face seems to show some understanding of what is happening to Germany. With Shatta Simon and her son Jean-Paul on the river bank by the bridge over the Tarn at Moissac in 1942 (below).

In love: Laure with Yitzhak at the Ulpan in Kibbutz Hatzor (above, left). A snapshot taken on a visit back to Moissac, Laure looking happy after telling Shatta about him (above, right). Laure, aged 79, with the author at her apartment in Courbevoie (below).

After *Kristallnacht*, when all the synagogues in Germany were destroyed by fire, the Nazis arrested 30,000 Jewish men (above) and threw them into concentration camps (below). Harry would have died there, had not Grete signed away all their possessions to get him released. The family had to leave Germany with nowhere to go and no money.

With Grete and Laure in Belgium, Harry was sent to the concentration camp at St Cyprien, near Perpignan in southern France. Grete had herself and Laure smuggled across two frontiers, to find the prisoners there living in damp tar-paper shacks. Those in the photo below are new arrivals. Harry was reduced to a walking skeleton. The camp suffered frequent sand-storms (above) to make the prisoners' lives even more miserable.

There were children of all ages in the French concentration camps along the Mediterranean littoral, clad in rags and some of them barefoot (above). But the worst thing was the barbed wire and the armed sentries guarding the perimeter (below).

Grete collapsed and died at St Cyprien. Ragged children (right) watched as her body was buried in the prisoners' cemetery. A prisoner's watercolour (below) records one departure to death camps. Even the two prisoners who died in the night have to be counted.

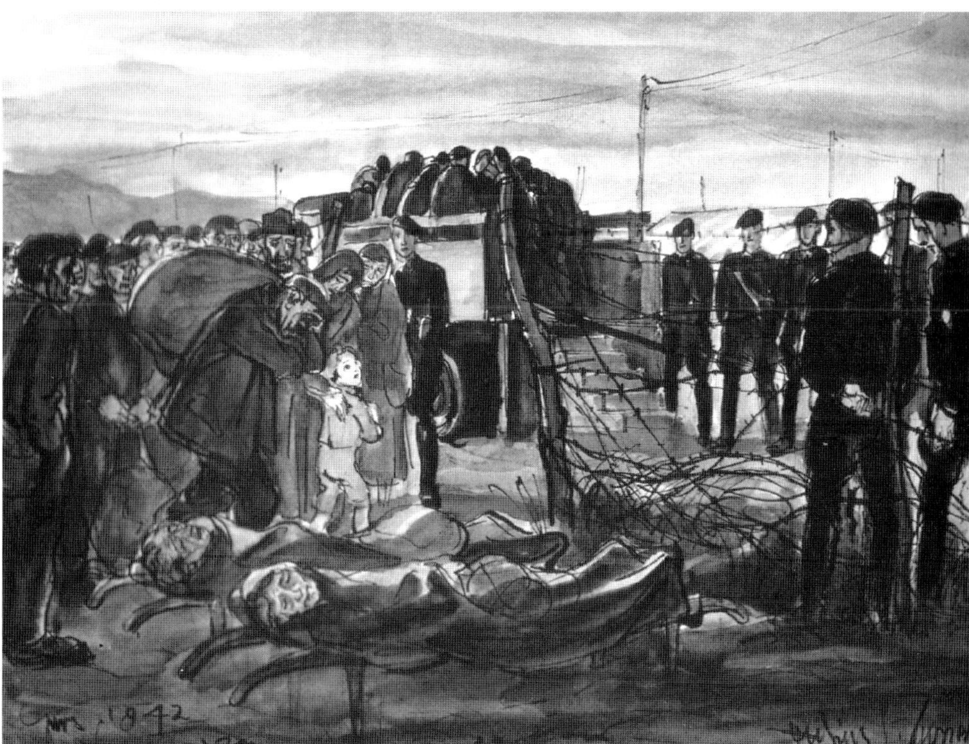

With sewage contaminating the drinking water, all the prisoners at St Cyprien were ill. Survivors were despatched in cattle trucks by rail to the other end of the Pyrenees. Gurs was the largest concentration camp in France (above and below), where Laure was separated from her father, placed in one of the men's blocks.

Destroyed after the war, the camp was as big as a town (above) with about 70,000 prisoners when Laure arrived in 1940. All that remains today is a small visitor centre and the understated memorial panel (below). Laure is mentioned nowhere. Smuggled into France with no papers, she did not exist.

In Gurs women, girls and male children under 16 lived apart from the men (prisoner's watercolour of women's barrack below). Their barracks were comparatively tidy, as the mothers were accustomed to doing housework. The men's barracks were not so well kept (above). It rained most days and the roofs leaked, needing scores of empty cans to catch the drips.

Between the heavy showers, there were lectures in the spaces between the barracks by university professors for the more educated prisoners (above) and school lessons for less educated adults and for children. Since Laure had no mother to nag her to attend 'school', she ran wild most of the time, searching for food

Some volunteer social workers were allowed into the camp at Gurs. Elsbeth Kasser (prisoner's sketched portrait left) was a Swiss-German veteran of this kind of work, who fed the starving children on Swiss milk and cheese. It is hard to recognise this post-war photo (below) of Elisabeth Hirsch as the smart and beautiful young woman who rescued Laure from the camp in 1941 ...

… and took her to la Maison de Moissac (right), a children's home by the river Tarn, where her sister Shatta risked her life with her husband 'Bouli' (below) to run an amazing rescue operation that defied the antisemitic government of Marshal Pétain, the Gestapo and the Allgemeine-SS to save more than 500 children's lives during the German occupation of France.

Shatta gave the children as normal a life as possible. In the mornings, those who could speak French walked to a local school (above). Life was organised as a Scout and Guide 'family'. Joining the Guides, Laure went camping (below) and found a new best friend to replace the one who had betrayed her in Berlin.

The first priority of children like Laure was learning French. They also had music lessons (above). Older boys were taught manual skills in the workshop (below) by local craftsmen. They were never betrayed by the people of Moissac.

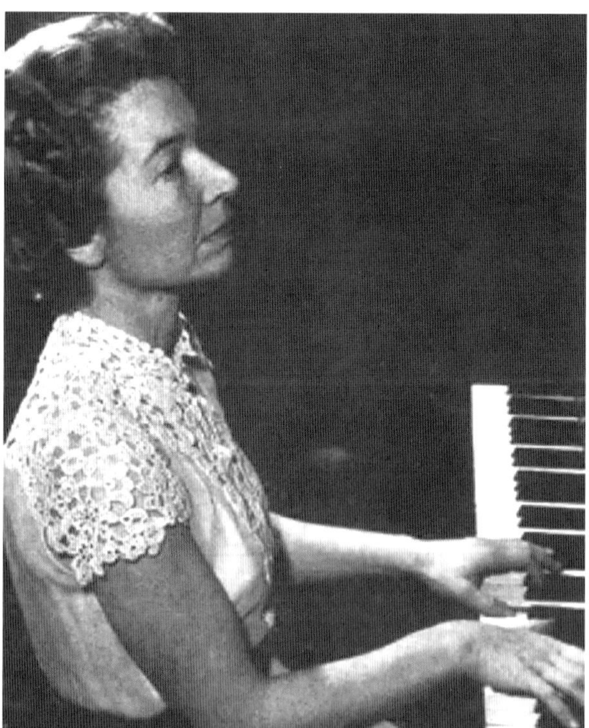

With the arrival of German troops in Moissac, Shatta's children had to be hidden in houses and farms all over the south of France. Laure was adopted by Hélène Gribenski (left) and her husband André. A famous piano recitalist (below), Hélène used music to staunch Laure's grief for the deaths of both parents in the camps, and became truly her 'living mother'.

the distance like a bad dream that would never leave them. At the railway station in Oloron they all got down, the lorry drove off back to the camp and Elisabeth led her four grimy children dressed in rags into the station café, ordering breakfast for everyone. For the children, simply sitting on a chair was a forgotten experience; there were none in the camp. Ravenous, they stuffed the bread rolls into their mouths and gulped down the coffee, with the result that they all had to run to the toilets, unable to digest real food following the long months of malnutrition. The toilets were upstairs, and Lore marvelled how clean the staircase was, compared to the filthy steps up to the latrines in the camp. After spending all day on trains – real trains with seats, not cattle trucks – they arrived in the evening of 8 May at their destination. Elisabeth had told her charges a little about the warm welcome that awaited them in the children's home to which they were going, but that meant nothing to their young minds so full of grief, apprehension, anguish and uncertainty. Would there be more food there? they wondered. Were there guards, or rats?

Chapter 11

The amazing Maison de Moissac

Most communes in France have some kind of subsidised accommodation for the homeless. In Moissac, a town of some 9,000 inhabitants some fifty miles west of Toulouse, this took the form of a spacious nineteenth-century house by the Napoleon bridge over the river Tarn. The official address was No. 18 Quai du Port.[1] On 5 December 1939 Shatta hired it indefinitely at a low rent because she thought its peaceful setting would provide a calm and healing environment for the displaced children she foresaw needing accommodation. Mayor Roger Delthil let her and Bouli in, showed them around, and handed them the keys.

Before the war, with a direct railway line to Paris, the town had been famous for growing sweet white grapes, sent north to the capital every day as delicacies. Today it welcomes thousands of people each year who come to visit the deservedly famous, richly decorated medieval cloisters. Situated in the so-called 'free' or southern zone, not occupied by the Germans, when the children from Gurs arrived there Moissac was controlled by Marshal Pétain's government in the former spa resort of Vichy. Vichy is a town that never recovered from the sigma of having been the capital of Pétain's collaborationist administration. The big hotels that had been full of people taking the waters before the war are now mostly empty or converted to other uses.

At first, Lore wondered where she really was and how she had got there. What made it afterwards nearly impossible to set down her first impressions of Moissac and the children's home is because gradually the place came to mean so much to her and inspired so much affection that it was like trying to describe the first meeting many years ago with a person who has become part of oneself. It was hard to remember that her real roots were elsewhere, that she only arrived in Moissac just before her thirteenth birthday, and that the little town on the banks of the peaceful river was not really where she was born.

When the four children arrived there on that mild, springtime Thursday evening, all they knew was that the Maison de Moissac was run by Elisabeth's sister, also a Romanian-born social worker, named Shatta Simon[2] and her French husband Edouard, nicknamed Bouli. The newcomers first saw her in the kitchen. Although she would now become what they called their 'living mother', replacing all the dead ones, she did not rush to embrace the new arrivals. It was not her style and she was aware that they were certainly carrying vermin and might have infectious diseases from the camps. Instead, she gave them all a heart-warming smile and welcomed them to what the townspeople of Moissac called 'the colony', like the *colonies de vacances*, to which French children were sent in the summer.

Then Shatta called Violette, the resident nurse. Finding it impossible to get rid of all Lore's hair lice any other way, she shaved Lore's head entirely and scrubbed *all* her scabies-itching body with a hard brush, making it bleed in several places before rubbing in a foul-smelling sulphur-based ointment, to kill the mites and their eggs. This was the only available treatment in those days, but the pain and the humiliation of being naked in the firm grip of the nurse, being treated like this, made Lore weep uncontrollably. Violette took no notice. Afterwards, Lore wondered whether she was really unfeeling or simply suppressing her sympathy in order to get the job done as swiftly and efficiently as possible. Then followed the two weeks of quarantine for all the new arrivals, in case they had brought with them some dangerous infection from the camps. Lore emerged ashamed of her hairless head, but many of the other children had shared her experience and took no noticc of this.

The four children from Gurs, with memories of the deprivation and horror of the camp still fresh in their minds, now found themselves in an incredible world of Scouts and Guides, where everyone used the familiar form *tu* for 'you' – even to Shatta and her husband Bouli. The house was part of the Jewish Scout movement. In France between the wars, everything had been organised on religious or political lines, so there were, for example, Jewish Scouts, Protestant Scouts, Catholic Scouts and even Socialist Scouts. This was, of course, against the teaching of Robert Baden-Powell, who had founded the movement with a prime rule embodied in his 1908 book *Scouting for Boys* that 'a Scout is a brother to every other Scout, of whatever country, class or creed'. The political and religious divisions of between-the-wars French society were what post-war president Charles de Gaulle most deplored about the deeply riven French nation of the 1930s which had, despite having the largest army in Europe, been so badly defeated in 1940.

The four recent arrivals were all wearing clean, fresh clothes – their old ones having been burnt. In her new clothes, after all the months wearing the same dirty, torn rags, Lore felt like the height of fashion. Her first meal with the other children was a Friday evening ritual meal. This was something she had never known, her parents being completely assimilated and not religious in any way. The other children singing in Hebrew, yet another language she could not understand, sounded bizarre to her ears. She was still finding it hard to communicate in French, which she had hardly ever heard in the camp at Gurs, filled as it was with foreigners. Since Shatta's and Bouli's rescue operation targeted Jewish children, who were most at risk, they were constantly coping with problems caused by newcomers who arrived by the railway from the north, wearing traditional black clothing, the boys having uncut *pais* side whiskers and imprudently talking Yiddish in the train, and by children of both sexes refusing to eat any food that was not kosher. One way or another, everybody in Moissac knew what was going on at Shatta and Bouli's refuge in the house by the bridge, yet they were never denounced. On the contrary, the local people formed a network of informers warning Shatta when Gestapo agents or Pétain's Milice set foot in the town, and some of the local tradesmen employed Shatta's older boys as apprentices.

A glimpse of the difficulties of running la Maison de Moissac can be gleaned from this extract from its archives preserved after the war at the château de Laversine.

> Roger – Father deported in August 1942. No known relatives.
>
> Isaac – Very sweet and affectionate little boy. Arrived in Moissac aged seven after being in Gurs and Rivesaltes concentration camps May 1940 – April 1942. Both parents deported in August 1942. No news of them since.
>
> Bella – Mother depressed since husband and son both shot. She refuses to take care of her daughter. The child has several times run away from her.
>
> Alfred – Unidentified orphan sent to us by Women's International Zionist Organisation.
>
> Léon – A good lad who wants to go into farming. He is to be sent to a rural group. He has one sister, who became insane after both parents' arrests.
>
> Hannah – Father caught in a *rafle* in Paris 1941. Escaped from Pithiviers concentration camp and clandestinely crossed into the Free Zone, reaching Moissac, where he worked as a tailor. Five months later, wife and children managed to join him here. In 1943 both parents caught in another *rafle*. Mother deported. Father escaped again, but was denounced. He escaped again, but was caught and sent to the mines. Caught by the Milice, he was taken to Drancy. During all this time, Hannah has been with us in Moissac.[3]

A *rafle* was a round-up, when German troops and collaborationist police units closed off a whole sector of a town or city, checked everyone's papers within the cordon and arrested all those who were carrying false papers or were obviously Jewish.

One of the first lessons for new arrivals at la Maison de Moissac was that the language of the house by the bridge was French, not German or Yiddish. There was no punishment for being caught speaking another language, in fact no punishment for anything. Lore was informed that her name was now Laure, pronounced pretty much the same, although spelled differently, in the French style. For the children like her who had suffered months of semi-starvation in concentration camps, it was like a dream, to be able to sit down on the benches in the dining room and eat their fill. With the strict rationing regulations and many children having no ration cards, the menu was primitive, based on large portions of *vesces*. These were a kind of lentil that would ordinarily have been fed to the pigs, but which tasted wonderful to the starving children, after all the months of grossly inadequate food they had been accustomed to. They also had to swallow a lot of charcoal, to get their damaged digestions working again. Like many of the children who believed they knew where a relative was imprisoned, Lore put aside a little of the food from each meal to send in small parcels to her father at the camp in Noé. These were the only presents the children could send to imprisoned parents.

La Maison de Moissac had its own Scout troop and Guide company. Once her hair began to grow again, Laure entered more easily into communal life, and was proud to be enrolled in the Guides, where the other girls in her patrol were her new sisters, all adoring the family atmosphere fostered by after-dinner singsongs, the Friday night dinners and festivals. Among outsiders who came to entertain the children was Marcel Mangel, who took his Resistance *nom de guerre* Marcel Marceau as his stage name when becoming an internationally famous mime artist after the war. Daytime at No 18 was as happy as Shatta could make it, while Bouli was the stern but caring housefather. In Laure's own words:

> In a sense, that first Friday evening marked the end of my childhood because, from then on, my own family life belonged to the past. From then on, there would be my

> substitute Moissac family and those two extraordinary people Shatta and Bouli, who were then so young and had a young son, and yet took the most enormous risks to protect us from death at the hands of the Gestapo. They also tried to do whatever was possible to heal the inner wounds we had suffered.
>
> There is no question but that Moissac was a strange world for a girl from an assimilated family who had hardly given a thought to God or being Jewish – and to whom all that side of life had negative connotations, like my rejection by Lieselotte, being expelled from school and Kristallnacht with all the synagogues burning. And like the Gestapo, Sachsenhausen and the endless fleeing and the concentration camp at Gurs. All those horrors that I had to bear without understanding the reason for them, had been inflicted on me just because I was born Jewish. And then, all of a sudden in Moissac with its same ancient rituals every week, I was in a community of which I could be – no, must be – proud. Most importantly, with the old life in ruins, I knew the joy of being part of a community.

The only less than pleasant thing in the house by the bridge was the obligatory daily dose of cod liver oil for each of the newcomers until they started to put on some weight. After months of incarceration, the children were amazed to discover that the front doors of No 18 and the overflow houses were never locked. They were free to come and go, but where could they go? At night, demons from the past haunted the dreams of the children. The problems the more disturbed children presented for their adult carers surpass the imagination.

From the camp at Noé Harry sent to Laure from time to time more of the pre-printed and censored cards with most lines crossed through, telling her that he had made friends with another prisoner named Apfel and that conditions in Noé were 'much better than at Gurs'. Particularly, he praised the small lending library in the camp, from which he borrowed books. She in return gave him all her news, the most important item being that she had a special friend! Sarah was the same age as her, and they became chums, spending their free time huddled together on a bench in the dining room, chatting like any couple of adolescent girls, untroubled by the din of the younger children playing all around them. Harry wrote back that he was delighted she had found a friend, and begging her to be polite at all times and show her gratitude to the management of la Maison de Moissac, and particularly to apply herself to her studies.

Had the circumstances been different, the father-daughter correspondence would have been like the letters from any parent to a daughter at boarding school, but Laure could read between the lines, and wrote to Herr Apfel, who gave her a truer picture: Harry's health was very delicate; it did not sound as though he would survive the following winter. In fact, of the 349 men and 252 women sent to Noé on 21 and 27 January 1941 nearly 200 died in the next few weeks. Without knowing the grim details, Lore was so worried that she requested a visit to him in the camp at Noé, although what she could have done there, except bid him a truly final farewell, she had no idea.

Like all the other children, Laure was expected to use the familiar second person pronoun *tu* even with Shatta and her husband Bouli. Since German also has a familiar form *Du*, she accepted this as part of the Scout ethic. Bouli acted as the house father, supervising the daily cleaning and tidying of dormitories and bedrooms and making sure each child turned the mattress over every morning to air it, as well as changing the bed linen regularly and sending any soiled clothing to the laundry. He also kept an eye on the older boys, who had outside instructors coming in to teach them useful workshop skills like metalwork and carpentry. Older girls taught the younger ones cooking and needlework. Laure – as she said of herself, 'a spoiled middle-class girl' – was amazed to see some of her new 'sisters' making new clothes for themselves and for each other. In one photograph of the girls at a summer Guide camp, it is touching to see how some of them have made themselve items of clothing or hats to wear. It was all the more amazing for her, since she had never seen Grete doing housework or with a needle and thread in her hands.

Although Lore's health was still precarious, it was such a relief to have her hair re-growing, although raggedly at first. She felt proud when Sarah wrote to her parents, far away in the north of France under house arrest *Ich habe eine neue Freundin und sie heist Laure* – I have a new friend called Laure. Sarah, her little brother Martin and her sister Ida were three gorgeous redheads, who had all been reunited at Moissac. And friends they stayed: at first Sarah and Laure; then Sarah, Ida, Martin and Laure. All three of the siblings grew up to become doctors after the war and were Laure's oldest friends on Earth. How could the bond born in the middle of that noisy dining room between two formerly traumatised young girls, ever be broken? Not since Liselotte had Laure had a real friend, and Liselotte had been the first to betray her.

Another great joy came when Laure joined the children's choir – not just because she enjoyed the new pleasure of singing, but also because she developed a crush on the charismatic older boy who conducted it. One of the older girls, called Marianne, who was eighteen or nineteen, gave French lessons to help her and some of the other young ones to learn the language of their new country. With Marianne's help and having language lessons also from Bouli's mother, who lived in the town, she progressed to the point where she was prematurely enrolled in the town's middle school and found herself lost among the local children, speaking too fast for her to follow and with strong regional accents. This resulted in the humiliation of being relegated to a younger class. The headmistress also decided that, in the time of permanent shortages of all food, her charges were in need of fattening-up. To remedy this, she doled out slices of bread soaked in cod liver oil to them all each day, disregarding Laure's pleas that she had already had the oil after breakfast, and standing over her charges until the school's oil-soaked bread had been swallowed to the last crumb.

By the nature of things, few visitors came to the house by the river, but one day in the summer of 1941 Laure and Sarah were sitting in the little square in front of the house, beneath the lime trees where some of the youngest girls were playing houses on the pavement with scaled down furniture that had been made for them by the older boys in the carpentry shop. A visibly distinguished gentleman and lady arrived. The two older girls had no idea who they were. Edmond Fleg was a famous Swiss-born philosopher, playwright, librettist, author and poet, who had fought in the French Foreign Legion during the First World War and been an active supporter of Captain Dreyfus. He was also Chief Scout of the Eclaireurs Israélites de France. His very elegant wife Madeleine talked with the girls sympathetically about their lives and, the next day, brought to Laure, yet again in the sick bay, a present. It was a book from a collection they were donating to the children in memory of their younger son, who had committed suicide in 1940, shortly after his elder brother was killed in uniform, fighting the German invasion. The book was entitled *Mademoiselle de la Seiglière*, and was the story of a girl from a good family falling in love with a count in the turmoil of the Revolution of 1789. Published in 1847, it was in the *genre* of 'improving literature' recommended for adolescent girls in Victorian times. Although revelling in this unexpected attention – when had she last received a gift? – Lore found the book too boring to actually read. Madame Fleg also asked her young friend to send her letters from time to time at an address in Beauvallon, near Cannes on the riviera. This was in the zone of southeast France occupied by Italian troops. Mussolini's administration refused to hand over Jews to the Germans, so the Flegs were hoping to keep out of the clutches of the Gestapo there for the duration of the war. Lore did write once or twice, but found Madame Fleg's replies couched in so literary a style that she could not understand them, although simply receiving a letter made her feel very important, which was doubtless her correspondent's intention.

As the months passed, Laure's health gradually became more normal and her stays in the sick bay less frequent. In February of 1942 she was informed that her request to visit Harry in the camp at Noé had been approved. On the day in question, she rose early, prepared a small parcel of edible presents and was about to head for the bedroom of the Guides mistress, who was to be her chaperone for the journey of several hours from Moissac to Zoé, when she was told that she had to go first to Shatta's room – not to her office, but to the private bedroom she shared with Bouli, which was very unusual. There, she was told that all visits to the camp at Zoé had been cancelled due to an epidemic among the prisoners. It was a crushing disappointment for Laure, and also a lie to protect her from the truth, which was that a small food parcel she had sent a few days earlier had been returned to Moissac marked *Adressee deceased.*

Many years later, Lore learned that Harry had died just a few days before all the prisoners then at Zoé were despatched to the transit camp at Drancy near Paris, and from there to Auschwitz. Since most of the inmates at Zoé had been old or chronically ill, it is unlikely that many of them would even survive the exhausting foodless journey to be gassed on arrival in the death camp. At least, she consoled herself, her father's death, coming when it did, had spared him the agony of dying during the long journey in filthy cattle trucks. From then on, Shatta refused to let any of her children enter a camp, for whatever reason. Even if Laure had managed to get to Zoé, she would at best have been able to see her father at a distance, the two of them separated by the double barrier fences of barbed with armed guards parolling between them.

Shatta's desire to protect Laure from learning of this new bereavement took the form of procuring an invitation from Edmond and Madeleine Fleg to go and stay with them for several weeks. Laure was uncertain about this. The Moissac House was now her home and the other girls and boys were her family. But she was given no choice in the matter and sat alone in the train from Moissac to Saint-Raphaël anguishing over what might be her reception in the Flegs' home. She had left Moissac with a parcel of sandwiches and fruit for the journey. Unable to bring herself to throw away the uneaten items or leave them on the train, she walked out of the station at Saint Raphaël clutching what remained. Seeing the Flegs waiting for her by their chauffeur-driven car, she realised that she was committing a *faux pas*. How could they understand that it was impossible for their young guest ever to throw any food away?

Set in a beautiful garden, their house was smothered in wisteria and filled with books and precious works of art. In terms of culture, it reminded Laure of her maiden great-aunts' house in Berlin, but it was somehow welcoming and comfortable too. Beside Edmond and his wife, there was Ayala, the widow of the son who had died fighting the Germans, as well as Rose the cook, who had been both the Fleg boys' nanny when they were young. Shown up to Ayala's bedroom, which she was to share, Laure was in awe of this beautiful, confident and well-dressed young woman, who, unlike her mother-in-law, did not talk down to the young visitor, but treated her as an equal, when she was not away, working under cover for the Resistance. The days went by in a whirl of activity and visits to interesting places bathed in the spring weather for which the Riviera was famous. The Flegs were perfectly aware that Harry was dead, but played their parts, pretending to post the daily letters which Laure wrote to him. Madeleine was in every sense a *grande dame*, the product of a very rich family and an elitist education, yet Laure gradually became aware that, in her own rather distant way, this fashionable lady cared about the teenager she called *'ma petite Laure'*. Edmond Fleg – real name Flegenheimer – had no problem accepting Laure as a grandchild, replacing the children of his sons, whom he would never know. Far from acting as a famous author, to Laure he swiftly became a replacement for that other kindly grandfather she had once known in Breslau.

With Ayala coming and going on her secret work for the Resistance, about which she could never talk, it was Rose the cook, with whom Laure spent most time. Sitting in the kitchen watching her preparing the meals and performing small tasks that had been entrusted to her, it was with Rose – and only with Rose – she could let herself go and talk freely about her experiences, tears flowing down her face. To her surprise, when she asked Rose one day about the Flegs' two sons, whom she had brought up, she saw the cook likewise crumple up and dissolve in tears. With the whole household taking such care of her in their different ways, the only moments when Laure was embarrassed were when they had famous guests to lunch and she used at the table some slang term picked up in the dining room at Moissac, causing a momentary silence of disapproving surprise from the visitors. At the end of her month's stay in the luxury of Beauvallon, in the railway station waiting for the train back to Moissac, Laure was assured by Edmond and Madeleine Fleg that they would never forget her. The biggest wrench was saying goodbye to Rose the cook, to whom she had bared her anguished heart, and who had reciprocated by sharing her own grief.

A couple of days after Laure's return to the Maison de Moissac, she was again summoned to Shatta's private bedroom, this time to be given the news that her father had died at Noé. The shock of this final deprivation was so profound that she kept no memory of it in her mind; it was simply too awful to know that she had no relatives in the whole world, never mind that Shatta assured this distraught adolescent girl she was as dear to her as her own young son, Jean-Claude, and would forever belong to the family of herself and Bouli. It was typical of Shatta that in 1943, when she was warned by the local police chief that her children were on a list of those to be arrested, she refused to stop organising their dispersion after her doctor's warning that the added work-load might cause her to lose the child she was carrying. She replied, 'What does one unborn child matter when thousands of living children are in danger of being killed?'

In July 1942 the Moissac Guide company were innocently enjoying their annual summer camp under canvas to the north of Moissac in the lovely hill country of the Corrèzes *département* when a messenger arrived by bicycle with the news that it was too dangerous for them to return to Moissac because agents of the Milice and the Gestapo had arrived in the town, to arrest everyone on their list. This must have been surprising news to the girls, so well had Shatta and Bouli and the other adults involved concealed from them the spate of war news, which was at that time of one German victory after another. The girls were split up into couples and small groups, to be lodged with new foster parents in different locations, and moved every few days. However, Laure's health was judged still too delicate for her to live a peripatetic existence. Instead, she was found a place at the Château de Chaumont. The nineteenth-century château, built by a Russian millionaire for his French mistress, a singer who came from the Creuse region, is now in ruins, but was at that time accommodating the girls from the Rothschild orphanage at Neuilly, as being a far safer place for them than their usual home just outside Paris. Inside the walls surrounding the Château de Chaumont the conditions were however hellish. In Laure's own words:

> I spent a month there. It was sufficient to open my eyes to what a real orphanage was like in the time of Dickens. All the girls had to wear uniform check dresses. Punishments for any infraction were severe and, so some of them told me, included beatings. Certainly, they were all terrified. Most of that awful month I spent huddled near to the entrance gate in the hope that someone would come and take me back to Moissac.

At the end of the month, all Shatta's girls and boys returned to Moissac at the same time, when it was judged that the immediate danger was past.[4]

Chapter 12

Hiding the children

Putting the unhappiness of the orphanage at the Château de Chaumont behind her, Laure was so happy to share with all her 'family' at the Maison de Moissac the joy of being together again. It was not to last. In November 1942 Allied forces landed at several places on Vichy-occupied territory of North Africa in what was called Operation TORCH. Although many of the Vichy-French defenders happily surrendered, some just to be out of the war and others because they detested the government of Marshal Pétain, elsewhere fighting broke out between loyal Vichy-French units attempting to repel the Allied invaders. Meanwhile, British and other Allied forces pushed in westwards from the war against Rommel in the Western Desert. The German High Command in Berlin did not rate the Vichy defenders in North Africa very highly and were proven right as the Allies squeezed in on them from both directions. Berlin rightly judged it too dangerous to leave the Mediterranean coast of France undefended by German force of arms now that the Allies would soon possess the whole North African littoral just across the Mediterranean. So, on the European side of the sea, Wehrmacht units were ordered to march, cycle and drive in motorised and horse-drawn transport across the demarcation line to occupy the entire 'free zone' which was re-designated 'the southern zone'. Accompanying them, inevitably, was the whole ghastly apparatus of the Gestapo and the Allgemeine-SS.

For an entire year, with Shatta and Bouli censoring any radio news, the children at Moissac were unaware of how things had changed, except that every so often a small group of their friends would disappear. These were the ones old enough and fit enough to be smuggled by Resistance volunteers across and through the mountains that marked the Swiss and Spanish borders, operations in which many of the guides, like Marianne, lost their lives, some betrayed by the very gendarmes they had paid to turn a blind eye.

During this time, Shatta and Bouli kept the rescue home going while the winds of war turned in favour of the Allies. After the battle of Stalingrad ended in a catastrophic defeat for the German invaders, Shatta travelled to Montauban, to beg the *préfet* François Martin for blank identity cards and ration cards. He refused on the grounds that he was a civil servant loyal to Marshal Pétain for whom such an act was treason. But she persisted, telling him that, when the war ended in a German defeat, people would remember his attitude and he would have to pay the price for his decision. Miraculously, this produced 150 blank identity cards. Back in Moissac, the mayor's secretary, Manuel Darrac, and his secretary, Alice Pelous, lent her the official stamp that validated every document so that it could be copied. In the house by the bridge, some of the older boys practised forging the adult handwriting on genuine ID cards, while others copied the official stamp exactly and used this to fashion their own rubber stamps from the soles of old shoes to use on the documents they were forging. Then they were in business, but 150 false identities were not enough.

Receiving orders to arrest 1,700 Jews shown as such on the census list, François Martin and his staff did everything possible to ensure that the people affected were warned. This was not simple, for one careless word could reveal him as the source of the warning. So many children were being moved long distances that Shatta had to attend a planning meeting with other organisers in the Hôtel des Alpes near to the main station in Grenoble. In the middle of the meeting, two Vichy policemen knocked on the door and quickly detected the false ID papers, for which the penalty was torture to uncover the source. Shatta kept her nerve and told them, 'Yes, they are false papers. But we are meeting here to try and save the lives of 200 Jewish children under threat of deportation. You must do what your conscience bids you.' After delivering a warning not to stay so close to the station again, the officers left, their intended victims breathed normally again and took the advice to heart.

In November 1943 they announced to all the children that the operation in Moissac was going to be 'suspended temporarily' and they would all be sent to live in secret with sympathisers until the end of the war, which they hoped could not be long in coming. What prompted this emergency move was the arrival in Moissac of seven German Gestapo agents. They had come to arrest a few rich refugees living in the town, at the same time seizing all their property and assets. When the Gestapo men presented themselves at the house by the bridge, Shatta was absent and Bouli was in charge of the office. As soon as friends in the town told her what was happening, she hurried back, for good reason. Bouli came from an old French family and was in the habit of making plain how much he despised all French traitors and their German masters alike.

Happily, Shatta returned with her diplomatic charm in time to greet the visitors before Bouli could insult them. They demanded a list of all the children she was looking after. She took from a drawer in her desk a completely fictitious list of names which she had prepared in anticipation of this moment and handed it over. As the Gestapo men left, one of them warned her that they would soon return with suitable transport to take away all the children. Was his warning intended to be helpful, or was he simply threatening? Before they could return with lorries, in which to kidnap the children, the rest of the emergency plan was put in train. A hundred or more hiding places had already been arranged – in schools, convents, farms and with families living in remote areas. The downside was that the stability the children had gained by living in a community at Moissac had to be forfeited – for no one knew how long.

In this lethal game of hide-and-seek, Laure was called to the library, to meet Monsieur Gribenski, an EIF scoutmaster who told her to call him André. She had no idea that he was by profession a famous neurophysiologist. Born in Paris, he had studied at Ulm in Germany and came from a Polish-Jewish family who had run a restaurant in the town of Suwałki in north-east Poland. It had been arranged by Shatta for him to take Laure to live with his family, consisting of himself, his wife Hélène and their 2-year-old daughter, plus his mother-in-law. They lived in a village called Montpezat d'Agenais, only a couple of hours by train and bus from Moissac. Having already learned that adopted children were not always welcomed by their host families, Laure made up her mind that evening, before even meeting the other members of the Gribenski family, that she would keep herself apart from them. To her damaged teenage mind, it seemed that the less they knew about her the less they could hurt her. Her antagonism to the whole idea of leaving the Maison de Moissac – the first place at which she had felt at home since Kristallnacht – softened a little when André informed her that he was taking two other girls from Moissac. One of the other girls was Laure's best friend, Sarah.

On the evening before the children departed in many different directions there was a leaving party. The mood was subdued, with the children wondering whether they would ever again all get together with the friends who had shared the greatest sorrows that children can experience and also, despite everything, shared so many joys and such strong friendship in Shatta's and Bouli's 'family' at Moissac. Also, they were shocked at last into an awareness of the very real danger in which they stood – a danger that required their very special community to be split up like this. In addition, Laure's over-active imagination had her wondering whether André's wife was as keen as he sounded to give a temporary home to the deeply troubled 15-year-old girl, which she realised she was. She still dreamed regularly that she was again trapped in the hell of hunger, vermin, filth and mud that was Gurs.

Would the Gribenski family treat her as a scullery maid and use her like Cinderella to do all the chores of the household? Would they shout at her and punish her for misdemeanours? The problem was that, although of an age labelled adolescence, she was emotionally still a child, carrying, in her own words, 'some very heavy baggage'. Although she had the intellectual and physical maturity of her fifteen years, emotionally she was far younger and more vulnerable – still a child, whose head was full of romantic ideas culled from the hotchpotch of reading matter in which she had taken refuge to escape from a real world that was often unbearable.

She made up her mind to behave herself and not cause problems for these people on whom she would be dependent, but that she would not open up her life to them because it was her bitter experience that, as soon as she became fond of people and perhaps came to love them, they would vanish from her life. Of course, it wasn't always their fault, but the result was the same. It had been so during all those years, one person after another, starting with that horrible girl Lieselotte in Charlottenburg. Laure had, passing through her head, a procession of all these people – not necessarily in order of their importance in her life. So she was deeply terrified on leaving Moissac next morning with Monsieur Gribenski, whom she had no intention of calling André, even if he was a scoutmaster. As to the two other girls travelling with her, Laure admired Sarah's strength and her determination to find her parents again at all costs, and to look after her younger sister and brother, but she knew she was not of the same calibre. Also, despite their still strong friendship, Sarah was religious and Laure could not share that essential element of her friend's life. Although she never discussed this with her friend, Laure could not reconcile any image of a godhead with the existence of Nazi Germany, the deaths of both her parents and her experience of the camps at St Cyprien and Gurs and the nightmare train journey between them.

During their journey together next morning in a normal civilian train, André explained that Sarah and Ruth would be boarding at the school they would all attend for lessons, but – and here again Shatta's especial care for Laure is evident – she would be living with him, his wife, mother-in-law and little daughter. The school they would all attend was not the local French school, where too many questions would be asked, but a very small private school run by two Swiss citizens, Monsieur and Madame Baumann, who had three children of their own at the school. There were only eleven pupils, all told. The Baumanns ran their little school according to the anthroposophical philosophy based on the writings of the philosopher-mystic Rudolf Steiner in a farm belonging to them called 'le petit Mouligné'. Although they had to know who the three new girls really were, André stressed that on no account were the Baumann children – Marguérite, Jurg and Ursula – or anybody else, to be told their true identities.

Alighting from the train at Agen, the nearest station to Montpezat, they were taken to the home of a very active member of the Resistance. Mother of another EIF scoutmaster like André Gribenski, Madame Kisler was a woman who seemed very old to the three girls but was probably only middle-aged. The untidiness of her chaotic kitchen caused them to exchange glances, eyebrows raised in surprise when they learned that this was where they were to be given their new, false identities. Thinking to put them at their ease, Madame Kisler offered them coffee made in a frying pan, which they found very weird although, at the time, Laure wondered whether this was because she used the yellow enamelled coffee pot standing on a shelf to hide incriminating papers in case her house was searched.

She was actually very disappointed that Madame Kisler was not young and glamorous like Ayala Fleg, but she afterwards came to realise that this untidy old woman was nevertheless a genuine heroine, risking her life to help strangers in danger. The new identity card she conjured up in the untidy kitchen and the ration book handed to Laure gave her the name Laurette Savari, a girl whose parents lived in Corsica. It was a good choice, for that island was already being invaded by the Allies, so the fictional Monsieur and Madame Savari's daughter could not return home until the end of the war – nor could anyone check on her identity until then. Keeping the same initials was usual; it accounted for any laundry markings on the girls' clothes, should they be searched. For the same reason, Sarah and Ruth became Simone and Régine.

Laure had imagined that the false ID papers would be conferred upon the girls in some very dramatic and mysterious way, with them having to swear on the Bible never to betray those who had helped to get them. She had picked up this idea from *The Three Musketeers* and other similar books, so it was rather a let-down, comparing these fantasies with the reality of Madame Kisler and her messy kitchen. Alas, there was no need to swear on the Bible and Madame Kisler was only an old lady – although doubtless less old than she seemed to the girls then. And they were only three young girls who were trying to stay alive like thousands of others at the time, and not romantic heroines fleeing their pursuers while themselves accomplishing spectacular deeds. Everything was very confusing.

Not for many years afterwards did Laure think about this wonderful woman who, in her kitchen, made false papers that saved hundreds of lives during the German occupation of France. She had the courage and quiet heroism of people who volunteer to become members of a group exposed to mortal danger at any moment. Laure never forgot her, nor the lesson learned that day. In those times, as always when oppression seems to triumph, it was often the most modest and least obviously impressive men and women who took the greatest risks, because for them it was the right thing to do, never mind that everyone else seemed to have forgotten all about right and wrong.

It was at Madame Kisler's house that André – this young man who was taking three girls into the Unknown – smiled at Laure for the first time since leaving Moissac. His smile seemed to comprehend everything: her terror, her grief, the anguish of being uprooted time after time, her uncertainty about the future and, especially, about meeting other strangers, even if they were his family. Never a talkative man, André smiled without saying much, but it was his disarming smile which was the beginning of the very strong bond that grew up between them.

Fortunately, Laure never had to use her cover story, for she was afraid she could not have told it very convincingly and would not have lasted five minutes of questioning by a persistent gendarme – even less by a brutal Gestapo thug. Many years later, she still marvelled at the optimism of the protectors who thought the stories might save the hidden children in the last resort. But what about the brave people looking after the little children, who understood nothing of what was going on and were likely not only to get their cover stories all muddled up but, also, with the innocence of the very young, to simply tell the truth?

In the bus travelling on to Montpezat, Laure recited to herself the details of her new identity, in case the bus should be stopped by police or the Pétainist Milice to check everyone's papers. At the same time, she reflected sadly that, having already lost everything else, she had now lost her own name too. The three girls agreed that their new identities were like new shoes that did not quite fit yet. The warm and comforting world Shatta created in the Maison de Moissac already seemed like a dream. This new person, Laurette Savari, was travelling to a new family she had never met, wondering whether it was possible that where she was going there would be people she had never met and who would like her, even just a little bit. Maybe, but how could she *know*?

Who am I really? Laure wondered. Where am I going? What will become of me? Even with a fair chance of escaping the Vichy Milice, the German Gestapo and Allgemeine-SS, what did the future hold for her? Would she one day go to school properly and eventually be capable of earning a living, instead of depending on other people and being despatched from one place to another like a parcel? Would she ever be able to stop fleeing? Would she ever find a place on earth to call her own? In the immediate future, was it possible that she would find people who would love her, even a little bit? Not from pity for the 'hidden orphan girl' they had agreed to look after temporarily, but because she was a person they would really like to know? Perhaps, but how could she know? Such were the confused and confusing jumble of thoughts of the silent girl sitting on that bus from Agen to Montpezat on the dark day of November 1943. She wrote later:

> If only I had known then that, when I stepped off the bus, I would be surrounded for the first time by my true adoptive family which would replace my dead parents and become totally mine, from that day on for the rest of my life. If someone had told me that on the evening when I arrived in Montpezat, I should certainly not have believed them.[1]

Such were the thoughts of the silent girl sitting on that bus, whose anguish outweighed her hopes by far, coming with André Gribenski and her two friends to the village of Montpezat in November 1943. If only she had known then that her understandable terror was unfounded and that, when she stepped off the bus, she would find a complete adoptive family, with a sister and later a brother, too, who became totally hers for the rest of her life. If anyone had told her that on the evening of her arrival she would not have believed them. Indeed, it was not true on the evening when she first met the three other members of André's family in that little house: his wife Hélène, toddler Martine and the grandmother. Hélène was a professional pianist with a beautiful smile and a sense of humour, but she talked very quickly and Laure, whose French was still hesitant, frequently had a problem understanding her. Both Hélène and her mother tried to put Laure/Laurette at her ease, but it was not easy for them since she refused to tell them anything of her past life, instead preserving a polite silence to any questions.

Martine, Hélène's little daughter whose bedroom Laure was to share, was at first the only person in whom she confided because she was only two years old and not yet able to talk and betray a confidence. But she loved being talked to by her new 'big sister' and clapped her hands with delight whenever she saw her. Laure's emotional problem was twofold: she desperately needed to be loved, but also to express love. Without realising that it was the thin end of an emotional wedge, she opened her heart to Martine, releasing the pent-up affection for a sibling that she had never been able to express before.

Weeks became months. Laure was never treated as a scullery maid, as she had so feared, but willingly helped to fetch water from the village pump – there was neither running water nor electricity in the cottage where the Gribenskis hoped to survive the occupation safely. She also accompanied André to buy provisions in the local shop, where the three girls' ration books made by Madame Kisler were accepted without question. Only during break-time at school, when alone with Simone and Régine, could she even dare remember that she had once had parents called Grete and Harry Schindler, and lived with them in the dreamland of faraway Charlottenburg.

The Baumanns' school was unlike any other she had attended, with so few pupils and only a handful of teachers. Putting aside his high academic qualifications, André taught the children basic mathematics and gave them an outline of the sciences. Hélène taught music and the history of music. The school's eclectic curriculum also included eurythmics – moving to music – and other subjects that had little to do with modern education. Another teacher whom the girls came to trust was 50-year-old Fred Berence, who taught art and the history of art, awakening in Laure a sense of wonderment that the human race she now knew to be so cruel could also create great beauty. Berence was a hypochondriac, swathed in scarves and surrounded by medicines, sometimes staying in bed all day and therefore giving the lessons in his bedroom. Yet, despite his obsession with mostly imaginary ailments, he was a tower of strength to André and Hélène and the only person outside their family and the Baumanns with whom they shared the knowledge of the three girls' true background. Laure summed up the whole curriculum of the Baumanns' school much later as being, with the exception of André's maths and science tuition, pretty useless as a preparation for university or a career.

Hélène and her mother may have expected Laure to trust them from the beginning but she would not let them penetrate her wall of silence. The grandmother, whom little Martine called 'Mamoune,' was a very beautiful woman who seemed very old to the new teenage member of the family. Although then not yet 50, her severe and rather morose appearance did nothing to encourage confidence. However, when Laure came to know her better she realised that behind Mamoune's sometimes harsh exterior was a wealth of goodness and true affection. It was nevertheless André who prised open the first chinks in Laure's psychological armour by talking as they walked home together from school. He was so patient, and seemed to expect nothing in return, whereas she could sense the impatience of the others for her to leave her world of silence and reveal her true self.

> Many years later, I realised that the simplest, the most natural and the best thing for all of us would have been to sit down with them and 'empty my heart' by recounting my life thus far. It would have been hard for them to understand at the time, and doubtless we should all have wept together, but the ice would have been broken, once and for all. As the adult that I am today, I know I should have done that, but the young girl I was then, really almost still a child, dared not do it, for fear of not being understood and certainly for fear of not being sufficiently loved to share with them all that pain and reveal my wounds that hurt so much.[2]

Only André somehow sensed that she needed time – a lot of time – and there was no point in pushing Laure. One of his most important characteristics was an unswerving respect for other people's personalities and needs. Although then quite young, he was already the man he would be all his life.

As can happen when one is young, after a few months living in Montpezat and attending the Baumanns' bizarre school, the girls accepted their lives as being a 'new normal'. Even Laure felt tempted at times to abandon her self-imposed barriers and confide in this family of which she felt herself becoming a part. As the long winter of 1943-44 ground on, she especially loved the evening poetry readings in which André indulged, by the light of an acetylene lamp, his love for the poems of Charles Péguy, a nineteenth-century writer who had died fighting as a reservist officer during the German invasion of France at the beginning of the First World War. However, to actually smash her carefully guarded barriers down completely would take a miracle, and one was on the way.

Chapter 13

The musical miracle

It came in the form of a Schubert sonata. Hélène being a professional musician, her playing was unlike the amateur playing of Grete on the grand piano in the drawing room of the apartment in Charlottenburg and Laure's awful weekly lessons with Frau Markoschewitz nagging her to practise between them. That all now seemed so long ago, like a dream in which all the details have been unclear. Accustomed to hearing Hélène playing the piano every day, Laure had instinctively shied away from consciously listening to the music, somehow sensing that possibly the emotion it could inspire might diminish her determination to keep her distance from everyone except little Martine.

Returning from school one afternoon, instead of going up to her bedroom, to be alone as usual, Laure sat down in the living room without any specific decision to open her heart and mind to deep emotion and began to listen to the real music created by Hélène's fingers as she played a Schubert sonata. Suddenly, without conscious thought and as though possessed, Laure found herself sobbing her heart out. This was not the weeping of a hurt child, but of an adolescent girl on the threshold of womanhood, weeping not just for herself and her sufferings, but for all the violence, cruelty and hatred in the world that contrasted with the beauty of the sound in which she was bathing. Many years later, she wrote of this moment:

> It was as if a wall shattered inside me, smashed to pieces by Schubert's music and Hélène's magical fingers. She stood up from the piano and wrapped her arms around me, saying nothing about the beauty of the music. Nor

> did she diminish the profundity of what was happening inside me with something like, 'Don't cry, little one. Everything will be all right in the end.'
>
> She made no attempt to console me, on the contrary holding me tight and saying in her contralto voice that was full of tenderness: 'Go on, Laure. Let it all out. Cry all you need to. It's high time. We were all beginning to despair of you and wonder whether there was anyone there behind all your polite silences. So go on. Don't stop. And if it will help you, I'll start playing again.'
>
> I understood that day that, if you cut yourself off from life and affection, you are dead. I understood also that one should never build a psychological wall to protect oneself against human feelings like tenderness and love, even at the risk of being wounded again and again.[1]

Hélène died in 1990. Several years later, the grief that caused Laure made it still the most grievous loss of her adult life. Since then, Laure had not had the courage to listen to 'her' Schubert sonata. Yet, she determined to listen to it again, knowing that it would make her weep, but not in the same way it had affected, in her words, the 'lost child' she had been on that evening in Montpezat, tearing her away from her self-imposed emotional isolation from life itself. Whether the psychological change for the better had something to do with it, who can say, but she felt her body starting to develop, as the long malnutrition in the camps which had prolonged her childhood gave way to a burgeoning of healthy optimism about the future.

It was in summer and autumn 1943 that the tide of war had at last turned against the Germans. On the Eastern Front an over-ambitious German offensive had resulted in the battle of the Kursk salient in south-west Russia becoming the biggest tank battle ever. There, 2,700 Wehrmacht and Waffen-SS tanks were destroyed or driven back westward by nearly twice as many Soviet tanks. Many of those were driven straight from the factories where they had been made to the front lines, picking up ammunition on the way. Operation HUSKY, the simultaneous British-American-Canadian invasion of Sicily, was to the German generals an obvious first step for the Allied invasion of the Italian mainland. code-named Operation BAYTOWN that took place on 3 September, followed by Operation AVALANCHE on the 9th. In anticipation of this, Hitler withdrew one-fifth of his armies in the east to safeguard German control over the Italian mainland and the Balkans. At this stage, his generals knew he had lost the war, even if he refused to believe it.

In May 1944 with whispered rumours all over the country of an imminent Allied invasion in the north of France, Laure's sixteenth birthday approached. Instead of being excited about this, she was unaccountably – to herself – depressed in a mood swing that she could not curb. She even sometimes suspected that the Gribenski family, who had been so wonderful with her since her arrival in their midst, were perhaps taking pity on her as a charitable activity and would quite possibly cut their bonds with her at the end of the war. Would they afterwards look back on her as a 'good work' they had performed for a girl orphaned by the war? Would the relationship dwindle to the exchange of cards or letters on special occasions? Confused by her inner turmoil and, due to her damaged self-esteem, doubting everything, she approached her birthday on 11 May unhappily.

She came downstairs that morning to find the whole family waiting for her. Hélène, her new pregnancy beginning to show, was seated at the piano playing *Heureuse Anniveraire* – as 'Happy Birthday' is known in France. On Laure's place at the table sat a birthday cake with lit candles. Only much later did she realise how grandmother Mamoune had been economising their meagre rations for weeks to save enough flour to make a small cake. And by the cake was a little present from each member of the family, including a drawing by Martine, which the birthday girl would keep and treasure. Looking at the table and the Gribenskis gathered round, Laure realised that, to them, she was truly one of the family. All her doubts about them and herself vanished in a flash. From time to time in later years, whenever her self-doubts resurfaced, she realised that it was not anyone else's fault, but her own, because no person who had lived through a childhood like hers could ever recover completely. Yet, inasmuch as any other 'war-wounded' young woman could be healed, she had been healed by their love. And this family that had welcomed her into its bosom and opened its hearts to her was indeed her family: mother, father, sister, grandmother – and soon a little brother to know and love.

Wonderful as this birthday revelation was, the shadows that lurked everywhere in occupied France suddenly lengthened. All that Laure knew at the time was that the whole family had to leave the cottage in Montpezat village and hide in a primitive two-room hovel deep in the forest. There was again no electricity or running water, but also no toilet. 'For that,' she told the author much later, 'we had to go into the bushes.' For the teenager who had survived the disgusting filth in the camp at Gurs, squatting in the bushes was perhaps not as awful as it might be for a modern young woman used to proper sanitation. What was awful for Laure, was the knowledge that hiding in the forest was necessary because 'some Germans' had come to Montpezat. She never knew exactly why this forced the family's move into the forest. As the author found during a visit to Montpezat in 2021, those Germans not only came to the village, but arrested, took away and sent to an extermination camp two Jewish men who had been hiding there for years without ever disturbing anyone or being betrayed by their neighbours.

This was the ultimate madness of the Holocaust. At the time when every German in uniform should have been fighting the Soviet forces on the Eastern Front, tens of thousands of Nazi soldiers and officials were turning their back on the Third Reich's real enemies to pursue the mad dreams of an insanely xenophobic ruler living in the fantasy world of his headquarters, hidden in the Masurian forest near distant Rastenburg in East Prussia. Perhaps even worse was that Himmler's Allgemeine-SS personnel, charged with sending their victims to the killing camps in the east, were hijacking with drawn weapons railway locomotives, carriages and trucks needed to transport to the western and eastern fronts the Wehrmacht troops and their urgent shipments of weapons and ammunition. After the millions of German soldiers killed fighting the advancing Red Army on the Eastern Front, half the men under Field Marshal Rommel's command awaiting the Allied invasion in Normandy were not even German, but Russian, Ukrainian, Polish, Hungarian and even Indian – turbaned Sikhs of the Japanese-supported Indian National Army[2] who had been captured in North Africa fighting with British forces against Rommel and then changed sides.

But, back to the hovel in the forest in south-west France. When the Gribs, as the three girls had christened them, moved with Laure into the forest, Sarah/Simone had been spirited away so quickly that Laure could not even say goodbye to her. She was now living with a peasant family in the country near Castelmoron-sur-Lot, who also owned the hovel in the forest. Ruth/Régine came with the Gribenskis and Laure to live in the forest until times were more settled. Six months pregnant, Hélène was now living in a temporary home that dated from the Middle Ages, with all the inconvenience that implies. Even obtaining provisions from the local shop required a person of courage and goodwill in the village to risk presenting their ration cards and bringing the food into the forest, avoiding hostile eyes, and leaving it in a place where André could safely collect it without animals finding it before him. He, Mamoune and Hélène slept in the smaller of the hovel's two rooms, with Ruth, Laure and Martine sleeping behind a curtain in the kitchen/living room.

It is impossible to imagine life in the hovel during the winter of 1943-44 with Martine learning to walk and talk and Hélène's belly swelling visibly while Mamoune did her best to make the scanty rations feed six hungry people. Laure and Ruth, with their bodies developing, without washing facilities or toilet paper and no feminine products – just some rags washed in cold water, wrung out by hand each month and hung on a string to dry over Mamoune's stove – had understandable spells of depression, followed by feelings of guilt for not showing more gratitude to their protectors. If Ruth could at least dream of one day being re-united with her family, Laure knew that was impossible for her. Her doubts were more basic. Would she ever be able to forget these terrible last years? Would someone ever love her, not as a child, but as a woman? Would she ever fall in love and have children? Would she ever even be able to study properly, pass exams, hold down a job and earn a living?

Although one might think that living hundreds of miles south of the English Channel guarantees warm winters, on the contrary, in the continental climate of south-west France it snows, it rains, it hails, it frosts and some days the freezing fog never melts. Gathering wood for the primitive stove, which was the only heating and on which Mamoune also had to do the cooking, was a labour shared: the girls collected kindling and fallen small branches and André carried or dragged back larger pieces of wood, all the time trying not to leave obvious trails in the snow leading to their hiding place. Afterwards, Laure could never recall how she and the other refugees in the forest learned of the D Day invasion of Normandy on 6 June 1944, but within a couple of days it seemed that everyone in France had heard the wonderful news. In a moment of poetry, Laure thought that these friends fighting and risking their lives daily in the north of the country had come 'to bring light into the evil night'.

French civilians thought that liberation of the whole of France would be a matter of days, but although the Wehrmacht generals were handicapped by Hitler's constant interference, their soldiers fought well, clinging tenaciously to each patch of ground against increasing odds. During this time, incautious optimists in France died by taking imprudent action against German troops. The leader of Free France, General Charles de Gaulle, had appointed General Pierre Koenig to be the officer commanding the Resistance – which was re-branded as *les Forces Françaises de l'Intérieur* (FFI). In broadcasts from Algiers and from London, Koenig tasked it with helping the invasion forces by attacking Germans all over France, and thus delaying their arrival at the battle fronts. Obediently, old men and young boys and girls with no military training unearthed a hidden firearm and went out to ambush Wehrmacht and Waffen-SS men, many battle-hardened by years of combat on the Eastern Front.

As bullet scars on buildings all over France still testify, the result, sadly, was often French bodies crumpled in a gutter. The home of a friend of the author in south-west France still has bullet scars on the front wall, testifying to the day in August 1944 when four local lads in a commandeered black Citroen *traction avant* with *FFI* painted in large white letters on both sides rounded the bend in the road to find themselves facing a German machine gun just 100 yards away. The boy driver must have been worthy of a race-track, had he lived long enough. He wrenched the wheel round, reversed back round the bend and executed a three-point turn before roaring back the way they had come. Managing to keep his distance from a pursuing German motor-bike with another machine gun mounted on the sidecar, he headed into narrow country lanes, hoping to lose the pursuers. The four lads might have got away, had they not met a German convoy heading in the opposite direction. Unable to pass them, they stopped, threw down their weapons and put up their hands. It made no difference. Beaten up, their hands tied behind them, they were strung up to the branches of trees and left dangling for their families to find them. A small memorial marks the spot on this quiet country lane. On the anniversaries of their deaths on that sunny August day in 1944 local people lay flowers on it as they do on similar sad memorials all over France.

In addition to the armies fighting in the north of France and the FFI men and women attacking Germans elsewhere, there was a third war in France at this time. Vichy French *miliciens* still loyal to Marshal Pétain rounded up fellow citizens *suspected* of Gaullist sympathies and murdered them, often after torture. Shortly after the Allied invasion of Normandy on 6 June 1944, Shatta told the mayor of Moissac to his face that, if he informed on *anyone*, he would be put up against a wall and shot when the Allies arrived. At the time, their arrival seemed like a matter of a few weeks away. In fact, Moissac was not liberated until 20 August and the mayor betrayed no one. Yet elsewhere, in the two months before Allied forces reached the area around Moissac and Montpezat, the deportation trains continued to shuttle away hidden adults and children from stations in Paris to the death camps in the east.

On 5 August Hélène gave birth to a son. Surely not in the hovel, deep in the forest, but we don't know where. Nor could Laure afterwards recall how long Hélène was in labour, or anything else about it, which suggests that she gave birth elsewhere. Afterwards, Laure could not take her eyes off this little person called Jean lying in the drawer that served as his cot, the first brother she had ever had. When he cried, it was from hunger or wind, not from grief or sadness. To the two teenage girls, he was both a miracle and a symbol of normal life returning.

On 25 August church bells all over liberated France – with the Germans still tenaciously hanging on in the east and north-east – were rung to signal the liberation of Paris, where in the very last days the city's police, which had collaborated *with* the occupying German forces for four years, took up arms against them and their hardline French sympathisers. People who changed sides at the end were labelled *résistants de dernière heure* – turncoats, in other words. Even as General de Gaulle led the victory procession down the Champs Elysées on 25 August, a few diehard snipers were still firing from high buildings into the crowds below. De Gaulle was the tallest person in the triumphant parade, making the easiest target. Afterwards, in his old office in the War Ministry, unchanged since the day he had walked out of it four years earlier, he admitted to one of his close supporters, 'Nobody could ever make me do that again!'

Unknown to most of his compatriots, it was not the Germans, but the Americans in the Allied invasion armies landed in Normandy, who had given him the most problems. US President Roosevelt's policy had been not to liberate France, but to occupy it as a defeated enemy power, which it never was, having been first an ally and then neutral, with the exception of the short-lived skirmishes in North Africa. Millions of francs in occupation money and postage stamps had been printed in advance in the USA. Had all that money been put into circulation by the Americans, inflation in France would have skyrocketed. In addition, hundreds of 'sixty-day wonders' – American civil affairs officers given a two-month course in the States thought to equip them to take over the civil administration of the whole country – were waiting to grab power for the Allied Military Government of Occupied Territory (AMGOT) as soon as the shooting stopped in each *département*. By dint of sheer force of personality and many sleepless nights, de Gaulle had blocked all the American plans, which would have caused a civil war, since hundreds of thousands of *résistants*, both the communists and others, had weapons and were not prepared to knuckle down under a new foreign occupier.

Roosevelt's punishment of de Gaulle's intransigeance was to forbid the leader of Free France to set foot in his own country. British Prime Minister Winston Churchill paid a lightning visit to Normandy on 12 June, when many of the D Day objectives had still not been reached after a week of hard fighting. On his return to London, he found the British newspapers accusing him of discourtesy in not including de Gaulle in his party visiting France. Without waiting for American or British permission, a haggard-looking de Gaulle landed in France on 14 June, his face betraying all the stress he was under at what should have been a moment of triumph. Forbidden to go back to his own country by Roosevelt and Eisenhower, he simply commandeered one of his own Free French destroyers to cross the Channel. Disembarking from *La Combattante* near Courseulles, he first visited the HQ of the Allied ground commander, General Montgomery, who was concerned at the plight of his 7th Armoured Division, being pushed southwards by German armour until the pressure was relieved. However, after a greeting that was courteous on both sides between Monty, dressed in baggy trousers and sweater devoid of insignia, and his tall, immaculately uniformed visitor, de Gaulle headed into Bayeux to install François Coulet as his first *Commissaire de la République* in the liberated areas. Coulet had been his *chef de cabinet* in 1941 and 1942, so de Gaulle knew him well enough to have complete confidence in the way he would handle the Allied Civil Affairs officers in liberated Normandy once he was installed.

One of Coulet's first acts was to disabuse the regional US Civil Affairs chief, Brigadier General Lewis, who assumed Coulet was, in some way, his subordinate. Refusing to call on Lewis, in order to establish from the outset the proper protocol, Coulet sent a message to inform the brigadier general that he would be delighted to receive him in his office. The reaction of other Civil Affairs officers in Normandy to Coulet and his small staff ranged from incomprehension to hostility. When Lewis came to call, he informed Coulet that he would tolerate his presence in Normandy until receipt of orders from his government clarifying the situation. Coulet spoke English well and had often served as de Gaulle's interpreter. He retorted with some force that he was there by order of the *Gouvernement Provisionel de la République Française* (GPRF) to uphold French sovereignty and thus needed no permission from Lewis or anyone else. Furthermore, he added that he was not so stupid as to hinder in any way the military operations in the region; his job was to re-start normal life for the civilian population that had suffered so much in the fighting. Lewis' manner changed immediately to protestations of sympathy and willingness to collaborate.[3] So much for the sixty-day wonders!

Allied radio stations in North Africa beaming transmissions into France were forbidden by Washington to refer to the Provisional Government, but the BBC did – an anomaly pointed out to the State Department by the British Embassy in Washington. As to the AMGOT currency, three days after the invasion, Churchill had cabled Roosevelt that de Gaulle was prepared to broadcast a declaration that this was legal tender but would almost certainly refer to the Provisional Government or 'la République Française'. When consulted by the President, the US Treasury Department indicated that, since nobody had yet guaranteed the AMGOT banknotes, de Gaulle could even denounce the notes as forgeries if he wanted to, in which case the Treasury would have to back them officially to the tune of $400 million! Since Roosevelt's chosen design did not look worthy of confidence and would have been easy to forge, the AMGOT notes were swiftly phased out. French civilians who had been paid with them for property or goods supplied to the invasion forces found it hard to get anyone else to accept what everyone called the 'forged notes'. They therefore used them for paying taxes, thus passing on to the authorities the problem of converting them into real money. Coulet instructed banks in the liberated areas to accept the AMGOT notes, but not put them back into circulation. In this way, by the end of August scarcely any were still in use.

De Gaulle's itinerary during his visit on 14 June took him to Bayeux for a walkabout through the ruined streets of the heavily bombed and shelled town and thence to Isigny-sur-Mer, where he shook hands with inhabitants who had survived the pre-invasion bombardments, conservatively estimated by the US government after the war as causing 12,000 deaths of French civilians.[4] He also made many brief and well-received speeches. If his face was unknown to the French public due to a rigorous censorship of any photographs of him by the Vichy authorities, his voice was well known all over France from all his broadcasts transmitted from London, starting on 18 June 1940. As his car was driving slowly along, a woman who had cut some flowers from her garden rushed up and threw the impromptu bouquet into his lap. Overcome with emotion, she called out, *'Vive le Maréchal!'* De Gaulle took this in his stride, remarking to his aide-de-camp, 'Yet another person who does not read the newspapers. Ah well, such is the force of habit. I'm sure she was a good Frenchwoman, all the same.' A parish priest rode up on his horse and rebuked the General for not shaking his hand earlier. De Gaulle got out to make amends, replying, 'I do not shake your hand, Monsieur le Curé. I embrace you.'[4]

On the voyage home, he boasted to officers on the bridge of *La Combattante* how the Americans with their AMGOT plans had been caught napping by the speed with which he had installed the first of the GPRF's civil administrators. To their voiced concern that the Allies would replace them with the Sixty-Day Wonders, he replied confidently, 'You'll see. They will say nothing and do nothing.'[5]

Chapter 14

The Good Germans

Of all the politics and squabbling between Washington and de Gaulle, Laure and her now increased family knew nothing, cut off from the world in the forest outside Montpezat. Even the continuing combats in north and north-east France and in the Rhône valley failed to concern her. Her ambition was to keep faith with all the other 'hidden children' and join them in Moissac as soon as it was safe to travel there. But when would it be safe? The retreat of the German forces in the region was not a neatly planned operation, but a chaos which could be fatally dangerous for civilians because many German soldiers were understandably trigger-happy. In several towns near Moissac, men in field-grey requisitioned all the bicycles so that they and as many of their comrades as possible could start on the long journey to the battlefronts in northern France. Adrien Favre, a friend of the author, answered a knock on the door one morning to find a *feldwebel* supervising the requisitions. Prepared to hand over his bicycle without argument, Adrien was staggered when the *feldwebel* instead saluted him and, having recognised him as the local schoolteacher, barked, '*Guten Tag, Herr Lehrer!*' He then yelled at his men in German to leave the teacher's bike alone. They might just as well have taken it because Adrien dared not let the neighbours see that his bike was the sole pair of wheels in the whole town exempted from the requisitioning, in case they thought he had been working for the Germans – the penalty for which could be death in those unsettled times.

In Moissac on the day of the town's liberation – Monday 20 August – there were some Wehrmacht trucks, into which the men of the garrison clambered, to be driven away, already aware that they were not being rescued but transported to the unwinnable battle in the north, where many would die. Nobody watched them go. The streets of the town were empty for good reason. Positioned outside the Carmelite monastery at the town's highest point was a team of three soldiers armed with an MG-42 machine gun in this commanding position that covered all the main streets, the slightest unwary movement in which brought down a hail of 7.92mm bullets that claimed the lives of the last Moissagais victims of the occupation. Even when the machine-gunners drove off in their Kubelwagen after all the trucks had departed, people hesitated to emerge from the shelter of their homes, in some cases for several hours, in case the men in field-grey came back, or other German troops passed through.

Nor was everyone safe even then. As one terror departed, another came out into the open. Frenchmen with rifles and handguns could now openly walk the streets, looking for those they perceived as having been collaborators. Some of these men were genuine *résistants*, others were posing as such, to cover up their previous inactivity. To show what brave and loyal Frenchmen they were, all over liberated France they took a sexual revenge on tens of thousands of women suspected, or known, to have had relations with a German. In Moissac, a 22-year-old, very beautiful hairdresser named Marie-Rose[1] had had a clandestine affair with an Austrian officer, who certainly had never wanted to fight for Hitler. It was not just a casual pick-up. They were in love and planned seriously to marry at the end of the war. Ordered to leave without being able to wish her goodbye, he had departed, she knew not for what destination, and she never saw her one true love again. Roughly arrested by men with guns on the Monday of the town's liberation and accused by them of *collaboration horizontale* – sleeping with the enemy – she was thrown with three other women into their temporary jail and locked up in the town's middle school under armed guard.

On the first Friday after the liberation of the town nearly all the hidden children managed to return for a celebration party with Shatta and Bouli in the house by the bridge – which had ironically been used in the meantime as a *Soldatenheim* for off-duty German soldiers. It must have been confusing for many of them, as it was for Laure. Were these boys and girls still her family, as they had been for so long, or was her family now the Gribenskis? Was it possible that only nine months had passed since she reluctantly left the house by the bridge? Then, she had been an insecure orphaned child from Corsica called Laurette Savari. Somehow, during the months of Hélène's pregnancy, she had left behind the doubts and fears of a child and now returned a young woman with her true identity: Lore, spelled French-style Laure, with her family name again Schindler. She sat alone in the bus and the train, retracing the journey with André and her two friends months before, having no idea that some people in Moissac were still suffering.

After two weeks of interrogations, Marie-Rose's whole body was bruised from beatings ostensibly to make her tell where a local *collabo* she had never met was hiding. There were lacerations all over her legs from the heavy, brass-covered butts of the interrogators' rifles. Two weeks after the German retreat, she and the three other young women under arrest – one was an 18-year-old prostitute from a *maison close* – were hauled out of the school and marched through the streets to the square in front of St Catherine's church, where a dais had been erected. Usually, prostitutes were left alone, since they had rented their bodies to Germans for payment, as sex-workers. So perhaps this unhappy young girl's crime was to have fallen in love with a client? On the dais, in front of a jeering crowd of men, women and even children, the four accused young women had their heads shaved to humiliate them.

Ordered to do this, a male colleague of Marie-Rose, who had been at school with her and ran a barbershop in the town, could not bring himself to shave off her beautifully styled hair. He handed his clippers to one of the men with guns, whose clumsy execution of the job added pain to her humiliation. The punishment was not yet over. The armed men shoved their shaven-headed victims off the dais and onto the back of a flatbed truck, on which they were paraded around the town with klaxon blaring to attract the maximum attention. The truck driver stopped deliberately in front of Marie-Rose's hairdressing salon, where several of her regular clients stood mutely watching. The only person with the courage to approach the girls was the mild-mannered little music teacher who had taught Marie-Rose at the *lycée*. Ignoring the rifles pointed at him, he took both her hands in his and said, '*Courage! Ça va bientôt se terminer.*' Bear up, it'll soon be over.

It was his courageous gesture of sympathy that broke the dam of her self-control. Tears streaming down her face, she was driven with the other shorn women back to the school and released four days later, at dawn before people were about, to face a walk of several miles back to her parents' house. A Spanish refugee from the civil war gave her a lift in his car for part of the way and tried to console her with the thought that people soon forget everything, both the good and the bad. That the Spaniard was right seemed proven when all her regular clients came back for shampoos, haircuts and perms and a whole crop of new customers booked appointments in an unspoken gesture of sympathy from the women of Moissac.

Recounting her experience to the author in 2006 in the company of a woman she had known all her life, Marie-Rose said she had never been able to talk about her humiliation to anyone else in all the six decades that had elapsed since it happened – not even to the man she eventually married. 'At least,' she finished, 'I knew how to make myself a wig. So I was luckier than many of the other *tondues*.' In that sense, she was fortunate, but came home years later to find her 6-year-old son by another man sitting in the salon totally bald. He had used her clippers to shave off all his hair. She never learned who had told him of her day of shame.

In nearby Auch, Renée de Monbrison and her children were staying in yet another of the borrowed homes they had known while on the run for the last four years. For several days they had been watching open trucks heading north carrying German wounded. On 19 August the German garrison drove out of the town with orders to re-group further north. One imagines the civilians at moments like this huddled in cellars, awaiting the ceasefire. Reality is so often more prosaic. Renée had packed the children off that day to the local swimming pool with sandwiches for a picnic and heard them come running back to the house yelling, 'Auch is liberated!' Her 18-year-old daughter Françoise, who spoke perfect English, jumped into the first Allied jeep to enter the town and kissed a wounded British liaison officer sitting in the rear seat, Captain T.A. Mellows. The other passsengers, Colonel Hilaire of the *Armée Secrète* and an American officer, also got a kiss, as did the Polish driver, before Françoise was told to get down and behave herself because they were there to kill Germans, not to be kissed by pretty girls.

Throughout her wanderings from one hiding place to another, Françoise's mother Rénée had kept intact her last packet of tea in the assumption that her liberators would be English and in need of a good cuppa. When she now proudly presented them with her precious gift, the result was laughter all round: tea was one thing they had aplenty. Despite the public relief in Auch that the enemy had gone, Mellows warned the family that they were not far away, having been halted at a barricade on the bridge over the river Gers at Isle-Jourdain manned by young men from a local Maquis group. Dusk came with a stalemate, the Germans unable to cross and the Maquis unable to prevail. After dark, the FFI *Armagnac Battalion* arrived and completely surrounded the German positions. At dawn, sporadic firing intensified until the arrival of the FFI *Corps Franc Pommiès*. Now outnumbered, the scattered groups of German surrendered, one by one.

Since that left no armed enemy forces in the *département* of Gers, everyone congratulated themselves on having liberated their part of France without Allied intervention. Groups of musicians were playing in the streets of Auch, with people of all ages dancing from sheer joy. For the de Monbrison family, the joy was tinged with sadness at the news that Captain Mellows had been wounded again – this time fatally – in a skirmish only a few miles away.

The war was not over. Fighting would continue in Belgium and the Netherlands, even after the last German troops had been driven out of France except for a few pockets of resistance. People of all ages would be starving throughout what they called *de honger winter* in the Netherlands, where the Wehrmacht had commandeered nearly all food for the people of the dwindling Reich. In December Hitler's last throw of the dice came in the form of the bloody breakthrough in the Ardennes, known as the Battle of the Bulge, which lasted five weeks, starting on 16 December 1944. At immense cost in lives, the German troops were all pushed back across the Hindenburg line by 25 January 1945. Yet the blinkered commander of the Nazi garrison in the French port of Dunkirk did not surrender until one day *after* VE Day, on 9 May 1945, after regularly hanging from the town hall for the crime of defeatism any men who dared to voice what was obvious to anyone – that Germany had already lost the war.

Instead of fearing the outside world as the war continued, Laure now knew she had her legitimate place in the world and wanted to complete an education that would permit her to go to university, earn a living and lead a full life as a free person. The only sadness for her and the other returnees was that so many of the people who had taken enormous risks to save their lives had lost their own. Their sacrifice, so Laure reasoned, imposed an obligation on her and the other 'hidden children' to lead full and happy lives in the future. At the beginning of the autumn term André secured a teaching position in Toulouse and the family moved there, to a rented house where Laure still shared a room with Martine, although spending half her time in Moissac. There, Shatta's steadily increasing family was far too big for the house by the bridge and the community had taken over a huge former flour mill on the bank of the river, not far away. There, Laure and her brothers and sisters from the house by the port found their family expanding with new arrivals from all over France.

Shatta was often absent, regularly travelling to Paris. There, at the Hôtel Lutetia on Boulevard Raspail, requisitioned by the Germans during the occupation years to serve as their headquarters for intelligence and counter-espionage, up to 2,000 returnees a day from all the previously German-occupied territories were processed. Seeking out children and young people whose families were dead and homes lost to them forever, she chaperoned them onto a train with her and brought them all back to Moissac. The country through which they travelled was still far from united.

Although the Germans had been driven out of most of France, the echoes of the occupation lingered, and all the previous frictions still fermented between the political activists of all hues. The *Parti Communiste Français* (PCF) re-invented itself as *le parti des fusillés* and claimed 75,000 martyrs shot by German firing squads, causing journalist Jean Galtier-Boissière to remark, 'Of 29,000 French victims of the occupation, we now learn that 75,000 were apparently PCF members!' Another PCF ploy was to label American MPs patrolling Paris in jeeps 'the new occupying power', but the need for military police was apparent, with the sub-prefect at le Havre recording rape, theft and violence by US troops that had put 300 women in the city's hospitals since June. Popular humour re-named SHAEF – the Supreme Headquarters, Allied Expeditionary Force – as the *Société Hotelière des Americains en France* because of all the luxury hotels and private houses it requisitioned.[2] Doctors and hospitals all over liberated France recorded the spread of sexually transmitted diseases on an unprecedented scale. The Wehrmacht had controlled brothels for all ranks and imposed regular medical examinations on the sex workers in them; the Americans pretended there was no need for this, with the result that there was an epidemic of gonorrhoea, syphilis and other sexually transmitted diseases.

On 31 August de Gaulle's provisional government moved from its headquarters in London and Algiers to Paris, holding its first combined Cabinet meeting there on 2 September, from which moment it had all the appearance of a legitimate government, although not an elected one. There was certainly no other contender for the title. On 9 September de Gaulle enlarged and re-shuffled his government. Although parts of the north-eastern *départements* would still be occupied at the end of the year and the German pockets of resistance around the major Atlantic coast ports of Lorient, St Nazaire and la Rochelle would hold out until the war in Europe ended on 8 May 1945, on 14 September de Gaulle began an exhausting series of visits to towns and cities all over the liberated areas. Like a medieval monarch showing himself to his people, he dismissed Pétainist civil servants and local government officers, and even Résistance heroes who displeased him, keeping in post men he considered irreplaceable for the moment. These included, as one example, Maurice Papon. He had organised the deportation of twelve shipments of Jews totalling 1,600 people from Bordeaux, where he was a sub-prefect, to Drancy and Auschwitz during July 1942 – and yet enjoyed a brilliant career post-war in the administration for more than half a century. Only in April 1998 was he sentenced to ten years' imprisonment for crimes against humanity but died in prison before his term was ended. A number of Communists were among those whose days of glory ended after a few minutes' conversation with the General; also, those in authority who had been too zealous in purging alleged collaborators. The priority, in de Gaulle's mind, was to re-establish order and weld his divided nation back into one people.

This meant an end to the freedom of action which many Resistance and Maquis groups had enjoyed. As early as 23 September most of the young men in the FFI found themselves conscripted as the head of France's provisional government made it clear that the war with Germany was not over and that their service to France would continue in uniform and under military discipline until it was. The strongest resistance to this policy came understandably from the *milices populaires.* Founded by the PCF initially as *milices ouvrières* or workers' militias, their numbers prompted Churchill to voice his unfounded fears in Quebec that September that Communist antipathy to de Gaulle would provoke civil war in France.[3] Roosevelt wrote to Cordell Hull on 19 September in justification of his continued non-recognition of the GPRF, now firmly established in Paris 'because it held no mandate from the people.'[4] Did he, in peaceful Washington, really believe that normal elections could have been held in a country where total war was still being fought and where several hundred thousand French citizens were trapped inside the German pockets of resistance?[5]

De Gaulle proved their fears ill-founded. On 30 October, under a deal made with the PCF, he pardoned and allowed to return to France the party's secretary-general, Maurice Thorez, who had spent the last five years safely in Moscow after deserting the French army during the phoney war. His deputy, Jacques Duclos, was anyway under strict instructions from Moscow not to cause problems for de Gaulle – who gave two posts in the provisional government to Communists – so long as his armed forces were fighting Germany and thus taking off some of the pressure on the Eastern Front. The ultimate compliance with Moscow came when PCF disarmed and disbanded its armed militias, the penalty for non-compliance being prison. And when Thorez returned to France in January 1945, he made a point of telling his followers not to rock the boat. 'We need,' he said, 'one state, one police force, one army.' To striking miners, he ordered, 'Roll up your sleeves and get on with the reconstruction of the nation.'

The programme of the GPRF included the establishment of special courts to try and sentence to death major collaborators and public figures of the Vichy regime. Energy resources including the coal mines were nationalised, as was the giant Renault motor company, the Gnome et Rhône aero-engine factory and the most important French airline, Air France. This was not socialism per se; as early as 18 June 1942 de Gaulle had announced in a speech at London's Royal Albert Hall that the propertied minority in France who had betrayed the nation and were profiting from the German occupation would be divested of their wealth after the war and promised that the masses who bore the brunt of the occupation should be rewarded after the eventual victory with a fairer share of the nation's wealth.

All this was a masterly show of authority by a leader who had yet to receive a single vote in a democratic election. Important as they were on the national and international scale, they passed completely over the head of young people like Laure, studying for her *bac* in Moissac.

Continuing her studies, so long interrupted, for the all-important *baccalauréat* exam that would lead to university, Laure tried not to think of the past, that wound still unhealed, as it was for so many of her friends, old and new, who had known similar horrors and were also trying to overcome them. In addition, she had worries quite normal for a young woman of her age. Was she intellectually strong enough to get the *bac* certificate after all the interruptions in her school career? Was she attractive to boys? Was she popular with other girls?

In the daytime, she sublimated all her doubts in study at the Moissac *lycée*, trying to make up for all the lost schooltime, but she also took part in all the activities at the Mill, especially the choir, still conducted by the same dynamic young man, on whom she had had a crush. Its repertoire included pieces by Bach, but also modern and traditional Hebrew songs and prayers. In the warm summer evenings, she joined in dancing the Israeli *hora* in a circle of young men and girls, all trying to forget the past.

In Bordeaux, the largest city of south-west France, a Kriegsmarine *feldwebel* from Dortmund named Heinz Stahlschmidt was the explosives artificer in charge of all the detonators required to set off the charges laid to render the port useless to the Allies. In peacetime a plumber who was also an Olympic-standard swimming champion, he had begun the war with three ships being sunk under him in two months, each time saving himself by swimming long distances to shore. Rewarded with an exemption from further service at sea, he had become a Kriegsmarine explosives expert. Stahlschmidt, a descendant of medieval Huguenot immigrants to Germany, was horrified by the order from Berlin to completely destroy all the waterfront of Bordeaux and its important buildings when the German garrison withdrew. He foresaw that the destruction of the port facilities alone would cause a tsunami effect on the wide Garonne river which would cost thousands of civilian lives. His religious upbringing did not countenance such an action, especially since (a) use of the port by the Allies was interdicted by the German pockets of resistance on both sides of the Gironde estuary, and (b) it was obvious to him that Germany was going to lose the war anyway.

He told the author,

> I was in charge of the demolition stores required to blow up all the important buildings in Bordeaux. When I asked a French docker to put me in contact with the Resistance, I met these guys who knew who I was and what was my job. They offered me 100,000 francs to destroy the demolition fuses stored in a heavily-guarded magazine in the Chartrons quarter of the town. Without the fuses, the charges were useless. I told them I didn't want the money. Instead, I wanted them to fix me up with a new identity, so that I could go underground and stay in Bordeaux with my French girlfriend when the Wehrmacht and Kriegsmarine troops pulled out. On the evening of 22 August 1944 at 20.15 hours I set off a charge that blew the magazine sky-high and killed about fifty German soldiers, wounding many more. After that, there was no going back.

Indeed not. The *Feldgendarmerie* (military police) were ordered to hunt him down and shoot him on sight but he had been whisked away by the Resistance, to be shuttled between the homes of members of a rugby team in the suburb of Bègles until the German withdrawal was complete.

However, the charges were still in place and some detonators had been stored elsewhere. So, on 23 August, in a typically Bordelais business deal, wine exporter Louis Eschenauer, who had sold wine worth 10 *million* francs to the Germans during the Occupation, agreed to talk to the German harbour-master who, in civilian life, was a Berlin wine importer with whom Eschenauer had done business for years, and with whom he lunched each week during the occupation of Bordeaux. This old colleague, Kriegsmarine Commander Kühnemann, agreed that the still possible destruction of large parts of the port was pointless since Allied use of the Gironde estuary was interdicted by the Royan pocket of resistance at the mouth of the estuary on the eastern side and another pocket at Soulac on the western side, at the tip of the Medoc peninsula.

Kühnemann disclosed the approach to his superior, German garrison commander Generalleutnant Nake, who shared this opinion, but had been ordered to carry out all the demolitions possible with what fuses remained. He in turn received an offer of a deal from the FFI – the official Resistance – through Gironde's Prefect, Maurice Sabatier, and Adrien Marquet, the socialist mayor of Bordeaux. This proposed that the Resistance would not harass the German withdrawal if the Wehrmacht and Kriegsmarine refrained from *any* demolition. General Nake himself dictated and had printed the following announcement:

> Notice to the population
> As supreme commander of German forces in the Bordeaux region, I declare that no destruction will take place in greater Bordeaux, and that the harbour and bridges which are mined will not be destroyed if the population refrains from all acts of sabotage in greater Bordeaux until the withdrawal from Bordeaux of all German forces.
> *(signed: Nake, Lt Gen, commanding 159th Division)*

On Saturday 26 August the notices were displayed throughout the city. It was on the reverse of one of them that the second stage of the deal was written by hand after being agreed between Kühnemann and Major Rougès, local commander of FFI:

> It is agreed as follows:
> All the German occupation forces must have left the city of Bordeaux by 2400 hrs on Sunday 27 August. The city, the port, port installations and bridges must remain

> intact. American and Allied troops and the Maquis may only occupy the city from 0001 hrs on 28 August 1944.
>
> *(signed) Commandant Rougès / Hafenkommandant Kühnemann.*

There was little more to it than that, apart from a few uneasy moments on both sides. In the early hours of 28 August Bordeaux was liberated bloodlessly shortly after the departure of General Nake's last troops. With his customary modesty, all Stahlschmidt said after emerging from hiding under his new identity as Henri Salmide to marry his French girlfriend was, 'It was the best thing I ever did.' Estimates based on the fighting withdrawal of German troops from Marseille and Grenoble on 23 August are that Stahlschmidt had saved the lives of at least 3,000 people in the city of Bordeaux and its port, German and French combined.[6]

He ended his interview with the author, 'I didn't return to Germany until twenty-seven years later, to explain my actions to the family. People there thought I was a traitor, you see.'

Towards the end of summer 1944 the whole Moissac choir travelled to Paris by train, using their real identities without fear at last, although the war was still grinding bloodily on and the British airborne troops at Arnhem were suffering 80 per cent casualties in Field Marshal Montgomery's over-ambitious drive to be 'first in Berlin'. Laure had previously had only a few glimpses of France's capital between the sacks of paper in the back of the people-smuggler's truck with Grete finding it difficult to breathe beside her. So, for a few days, she and the other Moissac youngsters who did not know Paris wandered through its ancient streets, finding a wonderland of history and monuments, including the thirteenth-century parish church of St Séverin and the magnificent medieval cathedral of Notre Dame, coming to know and love the city Hitler had ordered to be burned down and blown up as his forces withdrew. The order had courageously been ignored by General Dietrich von Choltitz, its last Wehrmacht commandant, who had also stopped what remained of Göring's Luftwaffe bombing the city by untruthfully telling him the bombs would be killing desperately needed German troops heading through it on their way to the next battle.

The plan was for the Moissac contingent to join with other choirs of children from all over France who had been saved from the Germans, to rehearse and perform what they called 'Le Gala de la Gratitude', a thanksgiving concert in honour of their saviours. This required much rehearsal before the great day in the largest Paris concert hall, the Salle Pleyel, which seated an audience of 2,000. On the evening of the concert, all the young singers were nervous, especially when they saw that the hall was packed with not a single empty seat. Somewhere in that vast crowd were André and Hélène, Laure knew, but she could not pick out their faces. The massed choirs on the platform overflowed the orchestra space, every single boy and girl determined to sing his or her heart out, not just for their saviours in the audience – whom Laure described as 'marvellous and heroic', but also to celebrate the life that had been given back to the hidden children despite *Hauptsturmführer* Danneker and his Holocaust colleagues, who had despatched from France 11,000 other children in the many French convoys to the death camps.

When they started to sing their thanks, Laure calmed down with the thought that she and all the others singing were the children of all the audience and indeed of all the people who had risked their lives. 'We were,' she said, 'not supposed to survive, but we were there that evening thanks to them. Never before and never again, I think, was there such a bond between the performers and the audience at a concert in the Salle Pleyel. Except that we were not performers and audience, but one enormous family.' The last item on the programme was *The Song of the Deported,* which began:

Loin dans l'infini s'étendent des grands prés marécageux
Où pas un seul oiseau ne chante dans les arbres secs et creux.

O terre de détresse où nous devons sans cesse piocher ...

The words could have been a description of the camp at Gurs.

> Stretching away to infinity are great muddy fields
>
> Where no bird sings among the dead trees
>
> O land of distress, where we are condemned to slave away without respite …

The last three lines of the song were:

> *Mais un jour dans notre vie, le printemps refleurira,*
>
> *Libre alors, ô ma patrie, je dirais tu es à moi,*
>
> *O terre enfin libre, où nous pourrons revivre, aimer, aimer.*
>
> But one day in our lives, spring will return
>
> And I will say, you are mine, O homeland, free at last,
>
> Where we can live again, and love, and love.

As Laure said to the author, many decades later,

> I will never forget all the audience standing up that evening and applauding. It should have been us applauding them, but they were doing it for us, saluting our survival and ability to sing in spite of all we had lived through, and despite the task that lay before us, rebuilding our lives without parents and with all the awful memories of times when we certainly had no reason to believe that spring would ever return.

Declared VE Day, standing for Victory in Europe, 8 May 1945 was just three days before Laure's seventeenth birthday. Church bells rang all the time in every French town and village. In the streets total strangers wept in each other's arms; others danced and sang at the news of the German capitulation. Yet Laure's memory of the day was confused.

> It was a wonderful day and I was seventeen, and had an obligation to be happy, despite what had happened to my parents. In my mind, I often spoke to Harry. That day, I remember saying to him, 'Oh, Vati, who can never know the joy all around me today, on the one hand there were the camps at Sachsenhausen, Rivesaltes, St Cyprien and Gurs and Noé and Auschwitz, but there was also Moissac and Montpezat and the wonderful people who saved your daughter and took her into their hearts after yours ceased to beat. So there is not just evil in the world, but also goodness, hope, generosity and love.[7]

Yet, she wanted to be alone because her feelings were so difficult to unravel. At the end of that school year, in the summer of 1945 André and Hélène departed for Paris to find an apartment where they could re-start their lives, leaving their two young children temporarily in Moissac with Mamoune, where Laure visited them often. But she preferred to sleep in her room at the Mill by the river where she was with other young people of her own age, planning a very different world from the one in which they had grown up.

Chapter 15

Where is home?

Laure passed her *baccalauréat* at the first attempt in the summer of 1947. Although she was then 20 years old, and thus a year older than the usual age to finish secondary school, it sounds like a near-incredible achievement for a student who had only learned French in her mid-teens after the horrific experiences of her childhood. The answer may be that, in 1968 after the student rebellion in France known as *les événements de mai*, when riot police confronted students burning cars in the streets of Paris and hurling torn-up cobble stones at them, President de Gaulle ordered his minister of education to pass every exam candidate as a way of defusing the unrest. So, as then head of the provisional government, it would have been typical of him to do the same previously in 1947 for the students traumatised by the experience of the German occupation.

Laure started life as a student in Paris while working in the daytime as a secretary to keep herself. Her subject at the Sorbonne was German language and literature, which may seem a strange choice for someone who had suffered as she had in her childhood and adolescence. In a sense she chose this discipline in a tribute to her father, who had so loved the literary treasures of the German language before his love of them was beaten out of him in Sachsenhausen.

After all the years being shielded from world events, she became aware during her years at the Sorbonne that momentous changes were taking place in the Middle East. Since 1922 the British had occupied the whole of Palestine under a mandate from the League of Nations after driving out the previous Ottoman occupiers during the First World War. Although this mandate embraced the Balfour Declaration, signed by Foreign Secretary Lord Balfour in November

1917, which declared Britain's intention to support the foundation of a 'national home for the Jewish people', in Palestine, most of the British Army officers stationed in the country were distinctly antisemitic and pro-Arab.

People at the time said this was because when those officers went into an Arab village and gave orders to the mayor – to repair a road, plant trees, dig a better well, or whatever – he followed the tradition of centuries of obsequious obedience to the previous Turkish overlords and always agreed with them: 'Yes, yes, *effendi*, that's a wonderful idea.' The British officers departed, happy with this expression of obedience. Nothing happened, of course. When the same officers went into the neighbouring Jewish village with the same instructions, the inhabitants, unfazed by men in European uniforms, replied with the famous Hebrew question *'Lama?'* Why should we have to do this? Why, indeed. And since the British had no answer, except that it was their plan, those villagers also did nothing. Of the two reactions, almost all the British overlords preferred the Arab one. Another part of the preference for the Arabs was, of course, that the officers tarred the Jews in Palestine with the same brush they had used on Jewish immigrants living in the East End of London and elsewhere in Britain. Most of them were descended from poor Jews who had fled pogroms in tsarist Russia and elsewhere. They lived in bad housing, made a poor living by menial work, spoke with funny accents and wore strange clothes.

There were some exceptional British officers in Palestine, of whom the most famous was the very religious Army intelligence officer Captain Orde Wingate, a literalist Christian who carried a Bible at all times and considered the implementation of the Balfour Declaration as the fulfilment of a Biblical duty. When posted to Palestine in 1936 at the time of the Great Arab Revolt led by the Grand Mufti Hajj Amin Al Husseini, who directed riots, massacres and nocturnal guerilla raids on the British petroleum pipeline from Iraq to the Mediterranean port of Haifa as well as on isolated Jewish farms and villages, Wingate's highly successful solution was to form the Special Night Squads (SNS). These were British-trained defence units that ambushed the raiders by night, using the same tactics of stealth that they employed. He based the SNS in Jewish settlements, knowing that his fellow officers would leak his plans to the Arabs if he stationed his men in British bases.

Whilst endearing him to the Jewish *Haganah*, whose leaders he trained personally, and who called him *hayedid*, meaning 'friend', it earned him the hostility of his superiors, who posted him back to Britain in May 1939, his service record reputedly marked 'Not to be re-admitted to Palestine'. Wingate went on to use similarly unorthodox methods in fighting the Japanese in Burma during the Second World War, of which the autonomous Chindit columns were the most famous and very costly in his soldiers' lives. Many of the men died from combat or tropical diseases, and Wingate himself died in a plane crash during a tropical storm near Imphal on 24 March 1944. There were a few other British officers in the last years of the Mandate sharing Wingate's feelings, but not many. One officer known to the author took his Israeli wife out to dinner in the northern port city of Haifa, leaving on the dressing table in their bedroom the key to a bunker in which a British field gun was securely locked. When they returned home after a very leisurely dinner, the key was in the same position, but the bunker was empty.

Towards the end of the Mandate, the Royal Navy in the eastern Mediterranean and the British Army on land were arresting all Jewish people, including survivors of the Holocaust, who tried to emigrate to Balfour's promised 'national home'. In a scandalous betrayal of men, women and children who had already suffered terribly in concentration and extermination camps under the Nazis, their new captors insisted on locking them up behind barbed wire in concentration camps on British-occupied Cyprus.

On 29 November 1947 the United Nations Organisation, which had replaced the League of Nations after the Second World War, adopted Resolution 181, which divided Palestine into a Jewish state and an Arab state in May 1948 when the Mandate was due to end. As the date approached, the Arab states surrounding Palestine threatened to attack and kill all the Jews in Israel as soon as the British occupation forces withdrew. Hitler would have been proud of them.

On 14 May 1948 David Ben Gurion, head of the Jewish Agency, proclaimed the state of Israel, which was recognised on the same day by the US President Harry Truman. Truman was the first head of state to recognise the partitioning of Palestine, enabling Ben Gurion to declare the existence of Israel. When asked why he had supported the Jews and not the Arabs, Truman is reported to have replied that, at the time, there were more than 5 million Jews with voting rights in the United States and very few Arabs in the USA who could vote for or against him. Often decisions of global importance are taken for domestic reasons, but it is rare for the head of a state or of a government to admit this.

Immediately, five Arab armies mobilised to invade the new country in a war which, in a sense, has never ceased. Israel's War of Independence pitted its small and poorly-equipped Israel Defence Forces (IDF) against five far larger and better-equipped armies from Egypt, Syria, Saudi Arabia, Lebanon, Iraq and the Jordanian Arab Legion, commanded since 1939 by the British lieutenant general, John Bagot Glubb.

The following day those armies invaded the UN-partitioned country with the expressed intention of 'driving the Jews into the sea'. Vastly outnumbered and using whatever armament they could acquire in a hurry, the native Israelis – roughly 20 per cent of the population of mandate Palestine – resisted. Since they numbered only 800,000 people of both sexes and all ages against more than 400 million Arabs surrounding them on all sides except the west, where the Mediterranean Sea was neutral, the Arab leaders severely underestimated their enemies' chances, overlooking the fact that the Israelis were desperate because they had nowhere else to which they could retreat. The Arab leaders also engaged in a conflict of interests with mutually antagonistic goals: Jordan and Iraq were Hashemite; Syria, Lebanon and Egypt were decidedly not. In what became known as Israel's War of Independence, the newly-formed, poorly-equipped IDF repelled the invaders in intermittent combats which lasted some fifteen months and claimed over 6,000 Israeli lives.

The eventual defeat of all the Arab armies after more than fourteen months of internecine squabbling and conflict with the Jews was blamed by them on the Jews being 'superior in numbers and equipment'. There were atrocities on both sides and many other complications in establishing the ceasefire line between the two communities in 1949, with several bottlenecks where Israel was only a few kilometres wide. Any soldier looking at the ceasefire map would have foreseen the consequently renewed hostilities which continued for years. Two fullscale wars erupted: the Six Day War in July 1967 and the Yom Kippur War in October 1973.

After completing her course in German language and literature, Laure had to face up to a difficult decision. All her previous changes of direction, except for going to university, had been imposed by force of circumstance. Now, as a new graduate, she had to decide where in the world she belonged. A return to the land of her birth was out of the question, with all her memories of terror and persecution there still fresh in her mind. In any case, no members of her family were still alive there. She was entitled to obtain French citizenship, but, although she had enjoyed her three years studying in Paris, did she *belong* there with her memories of St Cyprien and Gurs still open wounds? More or less coinciding with her final exams, a law was passed on 5 July 1950 by the Knesset – Israel's parliament – to be known as the Law of Return. It stated that *any* person of Jewish blood was entitled by inalienable right to emigrate to, and live and work in, the state of Israel. This clinched her decision to go to the only country that actually *wanted* her.

In 1952 Laure was already working for an organisation called Youth Aliyah. *Aliyah* in Hebrew means literally 'going up' but was used to mean immigration to the new state of Israel. To help young French-speaking Jews from North Africa travel safely to Israel, she acted as their chaperone. After Europe, the new country seemed chaotic, and her only knowledge of its official language Hebrew was in the songs she had learned on Friday evenings in the Maison de Moissac and the Mill. Yet, everywhere she went in this exciting new country there were residents with whom she could speak German or French and be understood. Perhaps what tipped the scale was the Israelis' determined and unapologetic lifestyle, everyone somehow beating a path through all the chaos to make new lives for themselves. Yet all the doubts she had about herself re-surfaced and made her uncertain whether she shared their strength of purpose and self-confidence. She was offered a position in Jerusalem with the *Alliance Française*, a worldwide organisation dedicated to the promotion of the French language and culture, in much the same way as the British Council does for English language and culture.

She returned to France and the familiar world of the community in Moissac, only to find that she had outgrown the need for its particular ambiance. Returning to Israel the following year to take up the job she had been offered with the *Alliance Française*, where her fluent French and German were useful, she swiftly realised that she should be learning Hebrew, of which her knowledge was quite inadequate. She headed for the Ulpan language school at Kibbutz Hatzor in southern Israel, paying for her keep by picking oranges in the orchards and working in the *bet yeladim*, where the children of the kibbutz were brought up, freeing both their parents for other work.

At the Ulpan she met a demobilised US serviceman called Yitzhak Levine, who was also studying Hebrew there. He had been an electronics student at the high-powered Technion technical university at Haifa in the north of the country. Before the year was out, on 31 December they were married. Life in Israel was pretty primitive in those early years and there was a constant fear of raids from Arab villages near the kibbutz or even fullscale incursions by the armies of the country's hostile neighbours. Both Laure and Yitzhak were determined to make a success of their lives at Kibbutz Hatzor but living there had its complications. There were constant arguments between the different factions in the kibbutz management: those who had been there before 1948 and those who came after independence. Even they were divided between those who had been hidden, especially by Christian families or institutions, and were constantly being savagely told by survivors of Auschwitz and the other Nazi extermination and concentration camps, 'You don't know what it was like there.' Well, certainly Laure knew what it had been like.

In 1960 Yitzhak decided to take his wife back with him to America, motivated by his dislike of what he termed 'kibbutz politics'. Laure was not at first sure about having to learn another language in a country with a very different way of life. Under the GI Bill, which provided some financial assistance to veterans of the Second World War, Yitzhak was entitled to continue his studies that had been interrupted by war service. The young couple left Israel and crossed the Atlantic so that he could take advantage of this provision. Laure did not really want to go. She had already known so many homelands: Germany, France, Israel. Why should she want another, and have yet another language to learn?

A couple of weeks after landing in New York, at the office of an organisation that helped immigrants to find jobs, she was asked what her ambition was in America. She replied that she hardly dared ask. 'So, what do you want,' her interviewer asked, 'to be an opera singer?' She answered that she would like to become a librarian. The reason for her choice was that she thought it would have made Harry happy to know she was surrounded every day by books as he had been in his library before the world turned upside down after he came out of Sachsenhausen.

Within a few weeks of that interview, she was working as a children's librarian for the Brooklyn Public Library. Swiftly picking up the vocabulary and grammar of her fourth language, she went on to become a reference librarian and eventually a branch librarian. This career with BPL lasted until she decided to retire in 1991. Before leaving America to return to France in May of that year she attended the First International Gathering of Children Hidden during World War II, held at New York's exclusive Marriott Marquis Hotel.

There, Nobel Prize winner and Holocaust publicist Eli Wiesel had told the 1,400 adults present who had been hidden children:

> You are the last links in a chain [of first-hand witnesses of the tragedies and atrocities that they had lived through]. When you die, it will be broken forever and people will not believe what happened. So you must tell your stories before you die. Who was the first hidden child? It was Moses. And since he was saved by a princess, each woman who saved one of you is a princess, and each man who saved one of you is a prince.

Wiesel foresaw that 'revisionists' would say that all the Holocaust stories were lies, never mind the memorials at Gurs and other camps *and* all the surviving documentation, including the photographs and films that were made at the time by the very perpetrators of a monstrous genocide. In that he was so right.

Romanian-born Wiesel had been deported from Hungarian Transylvania in May 1944, aged 15, and sent to the Nazi extermination camp at Auschwitz, where his mother and the youngest of his three sisters were gassed on arrival, the other two sisters and his father being murdered later. As the end of the war became increasingly obvious, Wiesel was sent on a death march westwards, during which any prisoner too exhausted to continue walking was shot, the body left at the side of the road. He stuck it out as far as the sinister camp at Buchenwald in central Germany, containing a quarter-million prisoners commanded by SS *Oberführer* Hermann Pister. On 11 April 1945 he ordered the commander of the nearby Luftwaffe base at Nohra to bomb the camp flat, killing all the prisoners. The order was refused. Pister cheated the hangman's noose by dying in Landsberg prison while awaiting trial.

In April 1945 Wiesel was liberated as a walking skeleton in the camp, where thousands of corpses lay unburied, by American Third Army troops. He began his writing career after ten years' studying in

Paris. In addition to fifteen novels and four stage plays, he eventually published more than 100 papers on the Holocaust and associated issues, which earned him honorary doctorates from many universities all over the world, including Harvard and Yale in the USA, Oxford and Cambridge in the UK, L'Ecole Normale Supérieur and the Sorbonne in France. He had been awarded the Grande Croix de la Légion d'Honneur and was also a Commander of the Order of the British Empire.

After the conference in New York, Laure tried to write her story in English, but knew as a librarian that it was not good enough. Yitzhak and a bilingual French friend produced different versions, which she also rejected. Her comfortable life in New York had begun to feel inappropriate for her since hearing of Hélène's death the previous year. So, after retiring from her job with Brooklyn Public Library, she moved back to France with Yitzhak. One morning after her return, she sat down to write her story and found that she was writing in French, something she had not done for almost half a century. Everything that had happened to her was still in her head – but in French. André Gribenski, also living in Paris, offered her regular help and advice and the book *L'Impossible Au Revoir* was accepted for publication.

Chapter 16

A strange visit

Laure hoped that a new generation in Germany would be trying to restore the country where the Shoah had originated to the nation that Harry had believed in – in her words, to repair the evil of the Hitler years. There were indeed children and grandchildren of the Nazi leaders who considered themselves guilty for what their parents or grandparents had done. Some of the women felt this guilt so strongly that they had themselves sterilised so that they could never give birth to another generation of the tainted bloodline they had inherited. Laure was also aware that there had been in Nazi Germany a few brave people who paid with their lives for fighting Himmler's empire of death, and fighting it in the most dangerous of places, the country where she had been born and which had rejected her. There was her outspoken nanny Anna and the brave Gentile friend of Harry who took him in after the horror of Kristallnacht and a political prisoner in Sachsenhausen concentration camp who gave his single blanket to Harry who was suffering terribly from the cold of the unheated barracks, the poor food and backbreaking labour.

Among the better-known German anti-Nazis were the circle of students known as *die weisse Rose* – the White Rose – formed in Munich around brother and sister Hans and Sophie Scholl. Sophie was a kindergarten teacher who printed thousands of denunciations of Nazi atrocities, which she stuck on walls and parked cars. She also risked immediate arrest by the Gestapo for distributing several thousand of her tracts in Munich's main station. As a child she had been obliged, like all German girls, to join the Bund Deutscher Mädel and Hans had no choice but to be a member of the Hitlerjugend – organisations designed by the Nazis to displace the Scouts and Guides in free countries. Taking a risk, because many parents were betrayed by their children, their devoutly Christian father told them not to believe anything they were told in school or by the youth movement leaders because the Nazis were murderous thugs who fed lies to all the children under their control.

After school Hans became a medical student and was drafted to the Eastern Front as a medical orderly, where he learned of the mass murders being perpetrated against not just Jews but people of many other non-German ethnicities. On his return to Munich, Sophie was horrified to learn from him the truth about the Eastern Front war, where Himmler's *Einsatzgruppen* followed the *Frontsoldaten* and killed hundreds of thousands of civilian men, women and children without any danger to themselves. The sixth tract published by *die weisse Rose* was addressed to the students of Munich university, inciting them to rebel before it was too late. Sophie and Hans released several thousand copies from the rooftops into the central courtyard of the university. They might just have got away with this incredibly brave act, except that the Nazi gatekeeper identified them and informed the principal, who interrogated them before handing them over to the Gestapo on 18 February 1943. They were immediately confined in Munich's Stadelheim prison – the largest in Germany.

Four days later the supreme judge of the *Volksgerichtshof* or 'people's court' travelled all the way from Berlin to preside over their trial. Roland Freisler was an insane lawyer, who abandoned any pretence of legal procedure and spent his time screaming with rage at the defendants. No one who appeared in front of him was pronounced innocent. Indeed, while Sophie and Hans were still being tried for 'high treason, subversive propaganda, complicity with the enemy and demoralisation of the armed forces', the Stadelheim prison guillotine was being readied for its grisly task by official executioner Johann Reichhart, the eighth generation of his family to hold the post. An appropriate associate for Freisler, Reichhart executed in his career 2,951 persons by guillotine and fifty-one by hanging. Of these, 250 were women. He later said that he had never seen a condemned person go to the guillotine more bravely than Sophie. Hans followed her a few minutes later and all their co-defendants were dead within a few hours of Freisler's no-appeal verdict.

So, yes, Laure was aware of the brave Germans who risked their lives, some losing them between 1933 and 1945 by denouncing Hitler's regime. But she only returned to Berlin shortly after the publication of the German version of her book titled *Der Unmögliche Abschied* in 2002 because her German publisher arranged a speaking tour for publicity. While in Berlin, she visited the streets of Charlottenburg which she had known as a little girl, finding the area remarkably little changed, despite all the new buildings in the nearby city centre replacing those flattened by British and American bombs in the Second World War. The house where she had lived was intact and she was able to visit the former Schindler family apartment, to find it had become a lawyer's offices. In the once familiar rooms, she could not decide whether this was a dream or a nightmare.

Walking along the corridor where she had invented an imaginary sister to play with so long ago, she came to the family kitchen where the lawyer's staff now took their coffee breaks. The former bedroom of Grete and Harry was the lawyer's prestigious personal office. He was in court that day but his bookcases were replete with learned tomes and every flat surface was loaded with stacks of paper relating to the cases he was currently handling. She had no need of a guide, but one of the secretaries insisted on explaining the current function of each room. Instead of listening to her, Laure was seeing and hearing ghosts, especially in what had been Harry's library where he had torn up and destroyed all his precious first editions after being released from Sachsenhausen. At the end of the tour she politely thanked the secretary who had shown her round and left. The lawyer's title to the apartment was watertight, being based on its transfer to the Nazi authorities under the laws then governing Germany, and she would not, in any case, have wanted to live in Charlottenburg again. After returning to France, Laure told the author.

> So I had gone back 'home' for a brief moment. But this was not my home. It was inhabited by strangers, who did not hear the tales those walls held for me. I could not hate them, for they had all been born after the war, but, whilst I was there, I felt a terrible grudge against them, which was completely irrational. I was like a soldier returning after a long war to find his wife married to another man and his house belonging to someone else. Going down the stairs to the ground floor, I said to my companion, whose presence had given me the courage to face this strange visit, 'So Hitler lost because I am still alive, to return here after fifty-six years.'

The German publisher had arranged a number of question-and-answer sessions for her with German secondary school pupils, who were respectful and seemed genuinely interested in what she had to say. Whilst one can never tell what is in another person's mind, she hoped their polite attention to what she had to tell them was indicative of a reversal of what had appeared to be a nationwide antisemitism during the Hitler years.

Chapter 17

The very last link

Berlin was a sad sight when the author was first posted there as a Cold War National Service RAF Russian linguist in 1958, snooping in real time on Soviet fighter pilots overflying Poland and what had become in October 1949 the Soviet puppet state known as the German Democratic Republic. True, the millions of tons of rubble from bombed buildings had been cleared from the streets largely by thousands of *Trummerfrauen* in their pretty summer dresses passing bricks and smaller rubble in buckets hand-to-hand because most German men of military age were dead or in PoW camps, where many of them were still dying. But that left whole areas flattened by the carpet bombing in raids by American bombers by day and the RAF at night. One could stand on what had been Adolf Hitler Platz and look all the way down the Kaiserdamm to the Potsdamer Platz more than two miles away without seeing a single building near this main throughfare. Judging by the sparse traffic, it could have been a quiet country road.

Being a natural solitary, ill-suited to military life with its lack of privacy, I explored the city alone on foot during my free time between duty shifts in the set room. One day, to my amazement, I came on the Charlottenburger Schloss – Berlin's answer to the Taj Mahal. This grand Baroque palace built by König Friedrich-Wilhelm I of Prussia was named for his queen-consort Sophie-Charlotte of Hannover – a sister of England's George I – after her death in 1705. Not content with that, Friedrich-Wilhelm gave her name to his whole estate, then outside the city, as Charlottenburg in memory of her. As the city expanded in the eighteenth and nineteenth centuries, this became a *Stadtviertel* of the Brandenburg capital. When I saw the palace standing so elegant and apparently undamaged, unlike nearby central Berlin, which had been flattened and made ugly by Allied bombing in the Second World War, it gave me some idea of what the German capital had been like before Hitler's insanity caused its almost total destruction in the war.

I had in 1958 no idea that I should, more than half a century later, be writing the story of a girl born between the world wars in Charlottenburg.

A historian is like a detective, digging up the past to find a clue here and another there. One of the bonuses of writing modern history is the additional possibility of tracking down and interviewing some of the people involved, to find out, not just what they did and what was done to them, but how they felt at the time. Were they brave or terrified, or both? Had they consciously chosen a course of action or felt they had no choice but to live through what was happening to them? And so on.

I first learned of la Maison de Moissac in 2006, when I was working on a history of the occupation of France.[1] Unlike the media representations of this period, which suggest, if they do not state outright, that the whole nation was composed of pro-German collaborators and anti-German Resistance heroes, I told the truth: that about 1 per cent of French people collaborated with the occupiers and about the same proportion were *résistants* who did everything possible to fight them. The remaining 98 per cent of the population just tried to live from day to day with all the shortages or total non-availability of foodstuffs, the power cuts, lack of fuel in winter and the plethora of regulations. Having read Laure Schindler's book *L'Impossible Au Revoir*, I wished to track her down and find out how anyone could adapt to a normal life after living through the hell of the concentration camp at Gurs and losing both her parents in two other French concentration camps.

Laure's French publisher said the company had no way of communicating with her, which did surprise me, since normally a publisher's accounts department has an address or bank account, to which royalties can be remitted. So, had they paid her an outright fee, instead of royalties? Such things can happen to one-book authors without an agent. My contacts in Moissac were unable to help because most of those whose lives were saved by Shatta and Bouli Simon had moved away or, like them, died during the six decades since the war ended. Then Chantal Fraïsse at the town's municipal archives gave me a telephone number for Jean-Claude Simon, their elder son whom I had only known as a cheeky little boy sticking out his tongue at the camera in a photograph of him with Shatta that was taken during the occupation. Chantal was not certain whether the number was still valid; he might have moved away from the address she had and in those days before mobile phones, be using a totally different number on another exchange.

I was in luck and delighted when I got through to Jean-Paul. He remembered Laure from the time when they had, as children, both lived in the Maison de Moissac, but he thought she had emigrated to either Israel or the United States after the war and was probably still there. The best help he could give me was to say that many of the now ageing former Moissac 'brothers and sisters' attended each other's funerals and he promised to see whether he could get any information on Laure at the next funeral gathering. True to his word, he called me a few months later and gave me a telephone number in the region of Paris. I called it and heard a very faint woman's voice answering. We were speaking French. To my question whether she was the author of *L'Impossible Au Revoir*, she replied that she was. It was very exciting, but I knew she must be elderly and might not wish to be bothered by questions from a historian unknown to her. She explained that she could not speak up because she suffered badly from Parkinson's disease, which is a long-term degenerative disease of the central nervous system. Sufferers of Parkinson's have a high risk of dementia, but clearly she did not have that problem: she spoke clearly and lucidly.

I explained my wish to write an English version of her book and suggested she could check on my credentials by looking at a list of my previous published works. Our first conversation was terminated as she had to go to a medical appointment, but not before she had agreed I could travel to Paris and interview her. That sounds very formal, but I wanted her to know and trust me.

Alas, a few days before the agreed date, I received a phone call, saying that her American husband had to go to New York and she wanted him present when we met. I completely understood. One often heard of elderly people conned into letting into their lives, and sometimes into their bank accounts, clever and unscrupulous crooks. So, having a witness to our meeting was no more than sensible. When we met at last, a few weeks later, in her modest but comfortable serviced apartment in Courbevoie, a north-western suburb of Paris, I already had a great sympathy for her, generated by reading her book. Of small stature, she was still the 'thinnest girl in the camp at Gurs'. Her physical health was visibly impaired, and any movement was painful but her mind worked normally. Also present was her American husband Yitzhak, slightly older than Laure. He apologised for causing the meeting to be delayed but explained that he had been informed that he had an inoperable brain cancer and not long to live. His trip to New York had been to bid farewell to his family there.

He was sitting on the settee holding Laure's hand at the time. Hearing him say that – which she obviously already knew – she confessed that, after the loss of her parents in the camps, she had always been anguished by having to say a final goodbye to anyone. Hence the title of her book which, in both French and German, translates as *the impossible goodbye*. I had the distinct impression that, when Yitzhak died, she would wish to go with him. The getting-to-know-you conversation drifted between French, English and German. When she mentioned that she had met Yitzhak in Israel, he said something in Hebrew. Not wishing them to think I was eavesdropping, I said, '*Ani medeber gam ksat ivrit.*' I also speak some Hebrew. 'I guess you are serious then,' Yitzhak chuckled. With death closing inexorably in on him, he had kept his sense of humour.

Having checked up on my previous publications, Laure was quite happy with my ability to author a version of her book for the English-speaking public. I explained that a simple translation would not be sufficient because there were many things which had not needed explanation to her French readership but did need to be clarified for an English-language readership. How many Anglo-Saxons even suspect that France had its own concentration camps in the Thirties and Forties? Laure and Yitzhak expressed themselves quite happy with the idea of me writing her story in English, especially after I told them of my two terms in 1946-47 when I attended a strange school at Otterden in Kent.

Almost all the other pupils were German refugees; I was one of only four token 'natives'. Although there was a headmaster called Dr Friedmann, the school was actually run by a tiny but very powerful woman, who had founded the school and made his life hell because she interfered in everything. That was Anna Essinger, known as *Tante* Anna, always accompanied by her sister whom we called *Tante* Paula. After working with the Quakers dealing with famine relief within Germany after the First World War, Anna set up a *Landschulheim* or boarding school at Herrlingen, just a few miles from her native town of Ulm in the German province of Baden-Württemberg. The town was later more famous as the home of Field Marshal Erwin Rommel. It was in Anna's former school, given to him as a family home by the Nazi government, that he was given the choice of committing suicide by taking poison brought by two SS officers, when accused of complicity in the July 1944 plot to kill Hitler. He agreed to kill himself so that he could be given a state funeral as a great German soldier, and his wife and son would benefit from a substantial 'hero's pension'. Had he refused to kill himself, he would have been tried by Friesler's 'people's court'. With his undoubted personal courage, he might have accepted that, and been sentenced automatically to death. However, the Nazi principle of *Sippenhaft* or responsibility of all the members of a criminal's family, would have his wife and son sent automatically to concentration or extermination camps. So, he swallowed the cyanide pill.

Correctly reading the writing on the wall after the coming to power of the Nazis in 1933, Anna Essinger transferred her school from Herrlingen to England. Some of the pupils arrived in Britain in the Kindertransport of the 1930s and others were still arriving when I was there, after they had been liberated by Allied troops from concentration and extermination camps in Germany and Eastern Europe during the closing stages of the Second World War. Many of these new arrivals were very disturbed, and one could understand why. Bed-wetting, even among the older teenagers, was common. Others stole food and hid it in their bunks, although they could eat their fill in the dining room at mealtimes and no questions asked. Many girls stole and hid items of clothing, although they could have them by simply asking. Bizarrely, the favourite game of the boys was *Selektion.* Each day, one of two rival gangs was nominated the SS gang. It drove the other gang into a barbed-wire enclosure in one corner of the school grounds, pretending to beat them with sticks, then went on to destroy the losers' camp. On the following day, the 'victims' became the SS. When I asked my best friend the origin of this 'game', all he said was that he had seen the real SS burn down his house.

One day I overheard Tante Anna tell him, *'Tommy, deine Mutter ist tot.'* With a precocious talent for languages, I had picked up German from the other children. Although they were supposed to speak English at all times and, at mealtimes, if she heard anyone using another language, Tante Anna would tap her knife against her glass and say, 'English, please!' I therefore understood that Tommy's mother had died. Walking through the school orchard a little later with him, I asked whether Tante Anna's news had made him sad. 'Everyone's mother is dead,' he shrugged.

When meeting Laure and Yitzhak in Courbevoie, I explained that I wanted no money from them for writing an English version of her book, nor was I offering to pay for permission to write my book. To avoid any subsequent misunderstanding, I had prepared a letter to this effect, which we all signed. What I most wanted at that stage were details of Laure's post-war life. How does a young woman, after a traumatic childhood like hers, settle down to a normal life in peacetime? How was it possible that, after her much interrupted education in German and French, Laure succeeded in getting her *baccalauréat* certificate and enjoyed student life at the Sorbonne university in Paris? Many students with even remotely similar histories abandon their advanced studies, yet she continued her studies in German literature, culminating in receiving her degree from the Sorbonne. There were so many questions to which I wanted answers.

While the conversation ranged far and wide, I noticed, displayed on every horizontal surface, many family pictures. Some were of Laure in Moissac or later, but there were also pre-war photos of Grete and Harry. How had she managed to find them? Frustratingly, the phone rang and I never had an answer to that. When Laure ended her telephone conversation, I asked permission to photograph these precious relics of her past life. Permission granted, I laid them in the sunlight on the balcony of their apartment which illuminated them well. For one reason or another, there were a few that I could not capture that way, so I asked – not really expecting a favourable reply – whether I might take these away with me to scan at home. Laure thought about it. I promised to send back by *courrier recommandé* – registered post – these few relics of her former family life, immediately after scanning them. She agreed, which is how so many photographs are reproduced here. It was a great gesture of trust on her part.

Many telephone conversations followed that first meeting. Then silence. I called the switchboard of the *résidence* in Courbevoie and was told that Laure and Yitzhak had moved away. I tried writing letters, with the envelopes marked *Veuillez rediriger* – please forward. They were returned, marked *adresse actuelle inconnue* – present address unknown.

I was left to guess that when Yitzhak's death was imminent, saying yet another goodbye – to him – was too much for Laure to bear. She had morphine tablets for her Parkinson's, so it would have been easy for them to drift away together after moving to some place where no one would try to contact them and inadvertently alert the emergency services, leading to possible re-animation in a hospital.

That is only conjecture based on my knowledge of her personal courage and determination, the key being the title of her book *L'Impossible Au Revoir*. She had been married to Yitzhak for half a century. How could she bid him farewell and live out her last years or months alone? Whether the guess is right or wrong, her disappearance left me as – to use Elie Wiesel's metaphor – the very last link in this particular chain.

Postscript

After the war, Shatta and Bouli continued their work for children and adolescents at the Château de Laversine near the town of Chantilly in the Oise *département* from 1951 to 1993. The elegant château, set in its own grounds, was formerly the country seat of the French branch of the banking family Rothschild. During the occupation of France, it had been the headquarters of the Nazi V-weapons staff supervising the construction, in bombproof tunnels within nearby quarries, of V.1 flying-bombs targeting London. Edouard (Bouli) first returned to his pre-war work as an electrical engineer before becoming involved in the Château, which the couple turned into a residential home for thirty-six boys and girls from problem homes, aged between 7 and 21. The extensive grounds offered opportunities for sports and, within the house, what is now called remedial teaching helped children who had, for whatever reason, dropped out of normal schools. An associated technical school provided training for apprenticeships in recognised professions. Shatta continued to direct the Château until retiring in 1990. Edouard died in 1993 at the age of 85. Shatta died in 2003 at the age of 93.

Elisabeth Hirsch found herself unable to return to France in 1945 because she had accompanied a group of children to Israel via Spain without bothering about getting herself any identity documents. In 1949 she succeeded in returning to Paris in order to direct the children's home called Le Refuge de Neuilly. She died in 1996 at the age of 83.

Hélène Gribenski returned to her life as a concert pianist after the war and also taught at the prestigious Conservatoire de Musique in Strasbourg. She died after a long illness in 1990 at the age of 72. André Gribenski resumed his teaching career as a professor of sensory neurophysiology at the University of Rouen and published several learned books.

Acknowledgements

Many people contributed memories and time to the research for this book. I first heard of la Maison de Moissac in 2006, when I was working on the *Dark Years* history of the German occupation of France. My neighbour Adrien Favre, who had lived through it all, gave me many details of everyday life. His English-born wife Joan reminded him of incidents he had omitted and told me of the work of Shatta Simon. Adrien and Joan introduced me to their friend Dédée Fourcassié, who had grown up in Moissac during the German occupation. She became my guide, philosopher and friend on the spot, introducing me in turn to people like the hairdresser Marie-Rose, who otherwise would never have talked to me about her love for her Austrian fiancé and her resultant suffering after the liberation of Moissac.

Thanks also to Dédée, Chantal Fraïsse welcomed me to the Archives Municipales de Moissac and shared its treasures. Also in Moissac, Dr Joseph Gouzi and his wife Paulette offered hospitality, shared memories of the war years and lent precious unpublished documentation. It was also Dédée who led me to her girlhood friend Françoise Blanchard, née de Monbrison, who unlocked the rich resource of her family's published and unpublished records of the occupation of Tarn-et-Garonne *département* just before Alzheimer's sadly wiped her own memory blank. Shatta's elder son Jean-Claude Simon not only found Laure's telephone number for me, but also made available photographs of la Maison de Moissac, so courageously directed by his parents.

In Paris, Naomi Wilson shared her research for a PhD thesis on women's experience of the German occupation. In Gironde, Christian

Chabrier, Jacques de le Bardonnie, Cathérine and Robert Hestin, the Marcellin family, and other neighbours and friends, opened memories of events that had not been spoken of for decades. The wife of Henri Salmide, formerly Heinz Stahlschmidt, put aside her grief and kept talking to me as he lay dying in Bordeaux. In Lot-et-Garonne, Guy de la Bardonnie generously shared both published and unpublished resources. In Charente-Maritime, Philippe Lelaurin opened the archives of his private, unsubsidised museum of the Second World War at Le Gua beside the oyster beds of La Seudre in Charente-Maritime. Sadly, his amazing collection of exhibits had to be auctioned off piecemeal later, due to lack of official support.

A big thank-you to Danna Messer, Laura Hirst, Lucy May and all at Pen and Sword Books.

My deepest gratitude goes to Laure Schindler and her American husband Yitzhak Levine for welcoming me into their lives and trusting me with their precious photographs and personal memories and feelings so near the end of their lives.

Douglas Boyd,
SW France, Summer 2023

Endnotes

Chapter 1: A strange reunion

1. Schindler-Lévine *L'impossible Au Revoir* Paris, L'Harmattan 2001, pp. 167-8

Chapter 2: Once upon a time

1. Quoted in C Laharie *Gurs, l'art derrière les barbelés* Biarritz, Atlantica 2007, pp. 154-6

Chapter 3: The night of broken glass

1. H-J Döscher, article in *L'Histoire* issue 274 of March 2003
2. Equivalent to £4 billion euros in modern terms
3. Horst Wessel was a so-called young Nazi 'martyr', dead for the cause. Two lines of the song are about 'Jewish blood spurting from the knife, which makes us feel so good'.
4. Lore was to meet her Oma and Tante Irma twenty years later, in Australia.

Chapter 4: Hitler breaks a promise

1. Report by Mike Lanchin on BBC World Service 13 May 2014

Chapter 5: Trust the German soldier

1. S.Winder *Lotharingia – a personal history of Europe's lost country* London, Picador 2019, p. 450 (abridged)

Chapter 6: News of Harry

1. H Schramm & B Vormeier *Vivre à Gurs* Paris, Maspero 1979, p. 51
2. *Basler Nachrichten*, 12 February 1941

Chapter 7: The nightmare of Gurs

1. *Encyclopedia of Camps and Ghettos in European Regimes Aligned with Nazi Germany* Vol III, published 2018 by USHMM / Indiana University, p. 152. This source is an impressive survey of the c.600 concentration and extermination camps in Europe and elsewhere.
2. To avoid Allied justice, Danneker wisely committed suicide in Bad Tolz on 10 December 1945, leaving a wife and two children who had to cope with sharing his bloodline.
3. See, in greater depth, D. Boyd *Voices from the Dark Years - the truth about Occupied France 1940–45* Stroud, Sutton Publishing 2007
4. C. Laharie *Le Camp de Gurs* Pau, Amicale du Camp de Gurs 1985, pp. 321-2
5. Schramm & Vormeier, p. 99
6. *Die Volksstimme* Swiss newspaper of 20 March 1941
7. In the Greek myth, Sisyphus was condemned by Zeus to spend his life rolling a huge boulder up a hill. Each time, before he reached the top, it rolled back all the way down and he had to start all over again.
8. Schramm & Vormeier, p. 54 (edited)
9. Footnote to p. 87 of C..Laharie *Le Camp de Gurs*

Chapter 8: Of lipstick, hairdos and passes

1. Ibid., pp. 15, 24, 25 (edited)
2. Schramm, & Vormeier, p. 119

Chapter 9: Mud, mosquitoes and music

1. M. Ludwig *Das Tagebuch des Hans O. Dokumente und Berichte über die Deportation und den Untergang der Heidelberger Juden* Heidelberg, Schneider 1965, pp. 16, 38

2. Unless otherwise noted information about the Gurs concentration camp is taken from Laharie's book *Le Camp de Gurs*.
3. Schramm & Vormeier, p. 120
4. Memoire of Elsbeth Kasser published in *Bulletin de l'Amicale du Camp de Gurs No. 38* (March 1990) pp. 3-6
5. Laharie *Le Camp de Gurs*, p. 350
6. Schramm & Vormeier, p. 119
7. Article by Dr Ludwig Mann, quoted *supra.*
8. Schramm & Vormeier, p. 51 (edited)
9. Archives départementales des Pyrénées Atlantiques M Prov. 500/12
10. See also Boyd *Dark Years,* pp.120-269

Chapter 10: Goodbye to Harry

1. Bulletin No. 19 (June 1997) of the Amicale de Gurs
2. Ibid.
3. Laharie *Le Camp de Gurs*, pp. 347-8
4. *L'Impossible Au Revoir,* pp. 103-4
5. Ludwig, p. 38

Chapter 11: The amazing Maison de Moissac

1. In post-war re-numbering, it became No. 2.
2. Shatta was born Charlotte Hirsch. The family came from Sighişoara, a walled medieval town in Romania. In addition to Charlotte and Elisabeth, their brother Sigismond was a radiologist in Paris, active in the Resistance. Deported in November 1943 to Auschwitz with his wife Berthe, she was gassed but he survived and returned to France. Their son Jean-Raphael was 10 years old when they were arrested. Already working as a courier, he was decorated after the liberation as the youngest member of the Resistance.
3. The names have all been changed to conceal the children's true identities.
4. *L'impossible Au Revoir*, p. 134

Chapter 12: Hiding the children

1. Ibid., p. 145
2. Ibid., p. 148

Chapter 13: The musical miracle

1. Ibid., pp. 152-4
2. Members of *Azad Hind Fauj*, the Indian National Army formed in 1941 by Subhas Chandra Bose to drive the British out of the sub-continent with the help of the Japanese.
3. M. Hella *L'Histoire du premier timbre de la Libération* in *L'Echo de la Timbrologie* September 2005, p. 28
4. E. Béthouart *Cinq années de l'Espérance* Paris, Plon 1968, p. 251
5. F. Kersaudy *De Gaule et Roosevelt – le duel au Sommet* Paris, Perrin 2006, p. 412

Chapter 14: The good Germans

1. name changed at her request
2. A. Beevor & A. Cooper *Paris after the Liberation* London, Hamish Hamilton 1994, pp. 20, 39, 117
3. Kersaudy, p. 283
4. Kersaudy, p. 384
5. Beevor & Cooper, p. 29
6. Boyd, *Voices from the Dark Years*, pp. 251-2
7. *L'Impossible Au Revoir*, p. 162

Chapter 17: The very last link in the chain

1. Boyd, *Voices from the Dark Years*